SANDY YOUNG
Postcard Memories

art in mixed media with kiln-formed glass

select works

by Sandy Young

www.sandyyoung.com

Cover: "Postcard Memories" by Sandy Young
Back Cover: Detail of "Postcard Memories"
This Page: Photo of wire behind kiln-formed glass.

Art & Design
by Sandy Young

www.sandyyoung.com

[STUDIO Y MEDIA]
PO Box 615
Sonoma, CA 95476

I express moments in time that not only represent the physical, but that include the inner experience, as well. My art offers portals and vistas into the arena ***where time compresses and expands, and where ideas, emotions and memories appear and disappear.***

this book

Postcard Memories

This book draws its title from my artwork of the same name. I've selected art pieces that reflect 19th century and early 20th century imagery and concepts of time. Postmarks, handwriting, book forms and early show posters serve as inspiration for the artworks included in this book.

These works of art are compositions of mixed media with kiln-formed glass overlay. Although not so readily apparent in photographs, each piece has a dimensional quality. Varying layers of color, transparency, paint and imagery in and on the glass interact with the imagery on the base panel to create a sense of depth.

My art expresses the multi-dimensional nature of individual experience as if traced over time through layers of imagery and markings.

I present most of the work on these pages with little commentary. The artworks based on show posters are the exception. For these, I give a brief description of the story behind each piece.

Typically, my art evolves organically from an initial inspiration or feeling. Only upon completion of an art piece do I develop a title and find my own meaning in the piece. I expect that the viewer, upon encountering a work of art, will bring a unique perspective and his/her own interpretation to the work. For that reason, I leave these open-ended. I intend for my art to reflect back to the viewer something that resonates within.

For artwork availability and up-to-date news and information, visit sandyyoung.com.

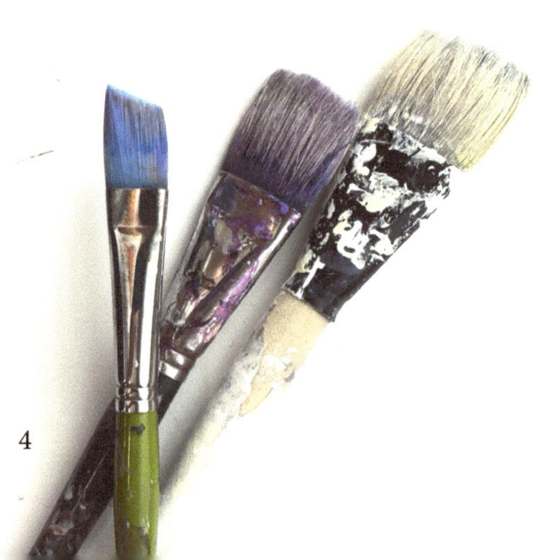

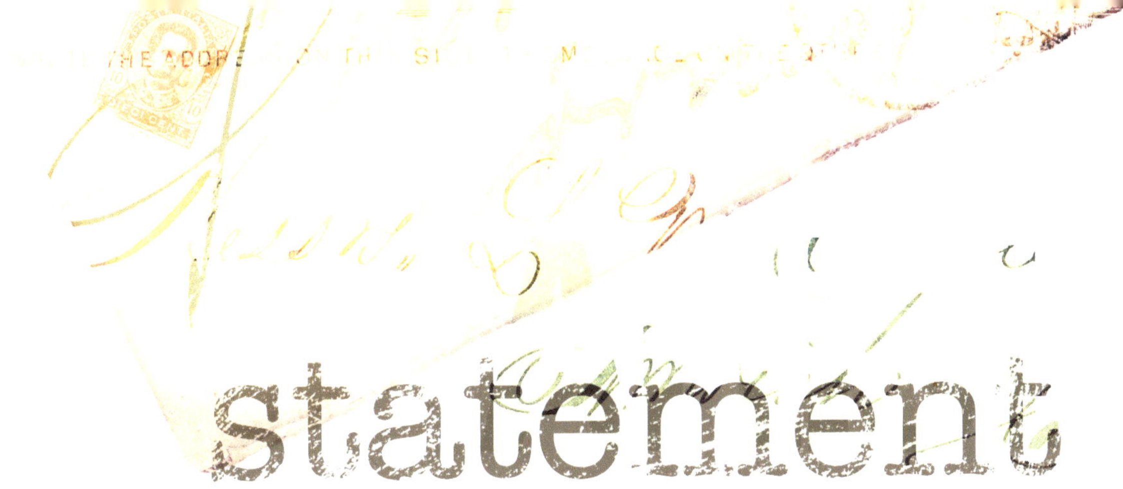

statement

As with memory, one moment is erased, while the next is painted, leaving only impressions of the first.

PALIMPSEST

(The second "p" is silent)

Definition:

(1) Writing material (as a parchment or tablet) used one or more times after earlier writing has been erased.

(2) Something having usually diverse layers or aspects apparent beneath the surface. Something that has many obvious stages or levels of meaning, development or history.

The word "palimpsest" comes from Latin palimpsēstus from Ancient Greek παλίμψηστος (palímpsestos, "scratched or scraped again"), literally meaning "scraped clean and used again".

I find resonance with the second definition of **palimpsest** where I am creating "*...something that has many layers or aspects beneath the surface... many obvious stages or levels of meaning...*" To that, I add dimensionality.

I weave imagery into multiple planes in order to create a feeling of dimensionality. This aspect of my work also serves as a metaphor for the multi-dimensional nature of individual life experience. Markings and handwriting symbolically represent tracings of internal experience. Distressed and fragmented layers allude to the passage of time. As with memory, one moment is erased, while the next is painted, leaving only impressions of the first.

I am often inspired by turn-of-the-century photographs, handwritten documents and time worn objects. I see these as evidence of someone or something gone before, and use them to convey a timelessness. Mixing old with new, combining disparate images and elements, I seek to create harmony and express a connectivity among all.

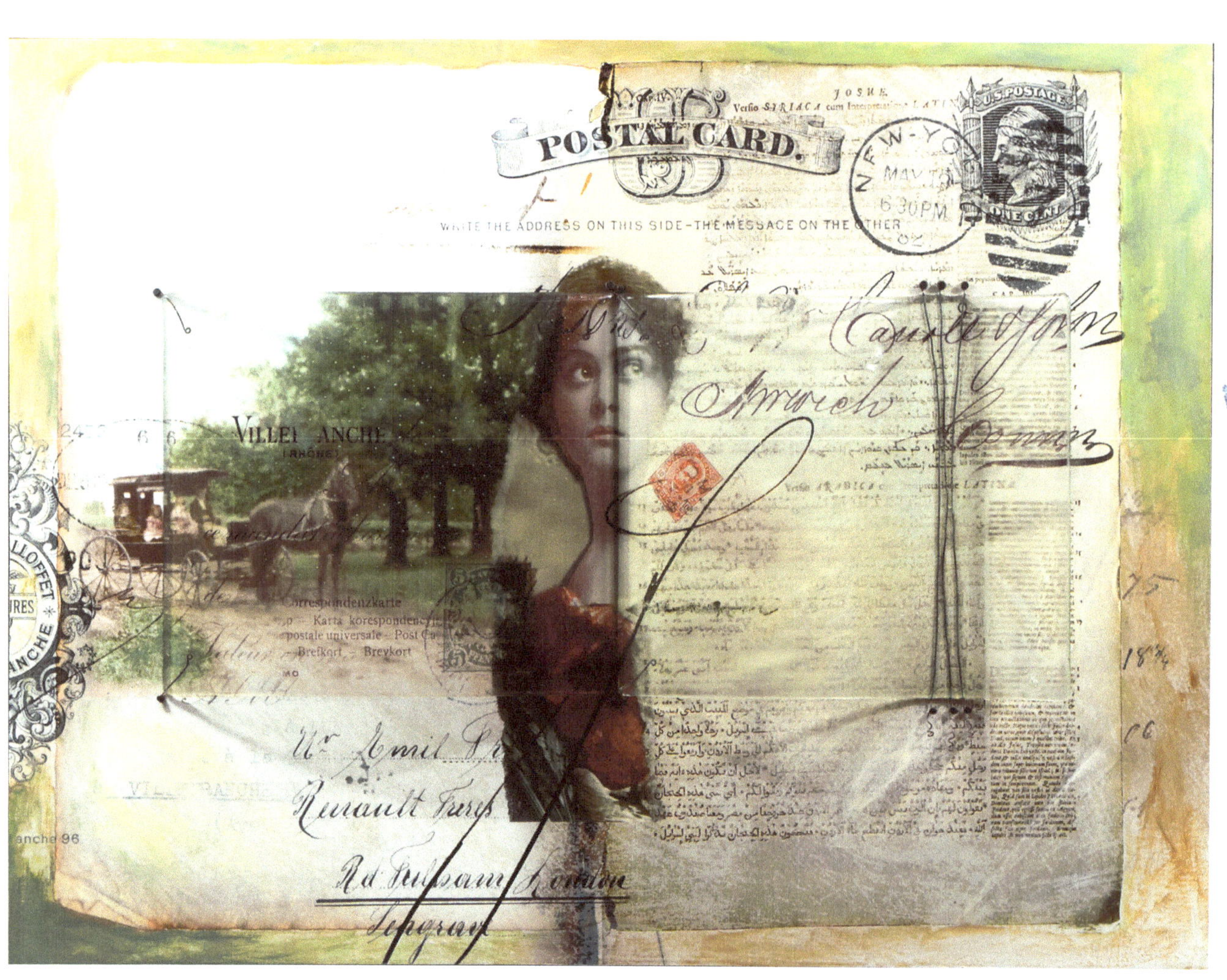

Postcard Memories

Sandy Young

mixed media with kiln-formed glass, wire, tacks, on birch panel

30" x 40" x 3" (2012)

Memories

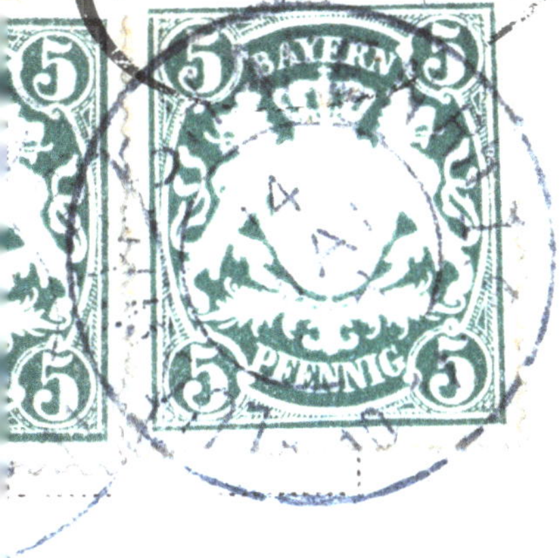

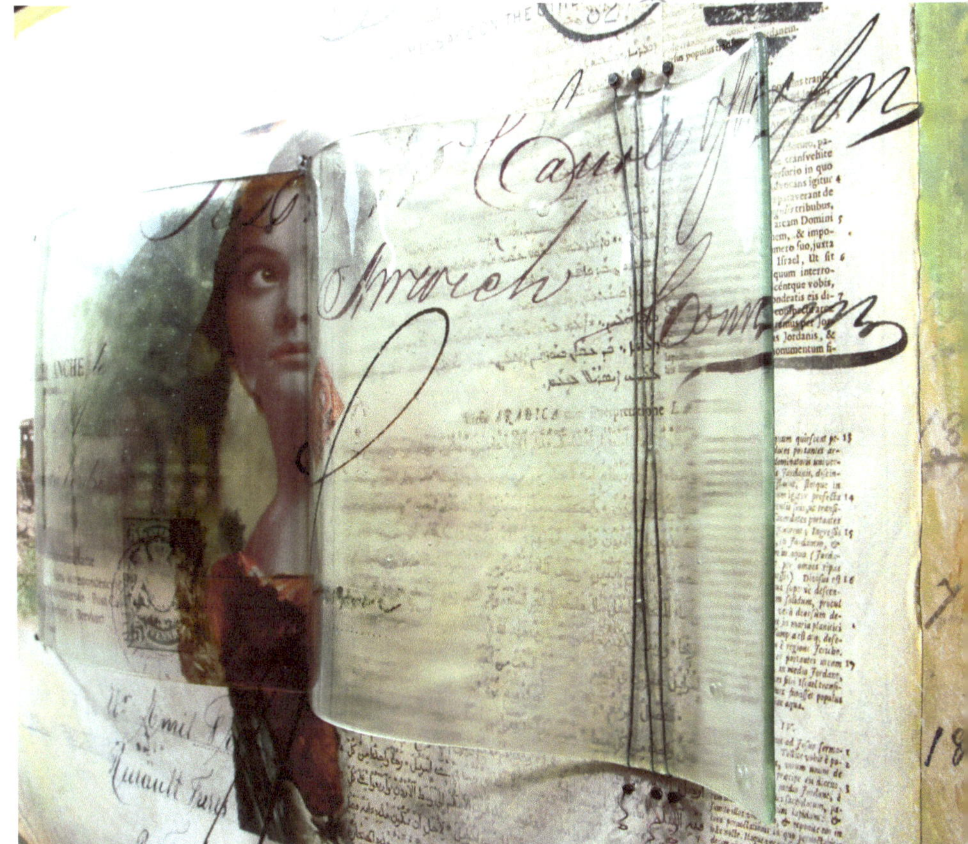

Right: Detail of "Postcard Memories" viewed from an angle showing the curvature of the glass overlay. The wires within the glass, along with tacks, anchor the glass to the panel.

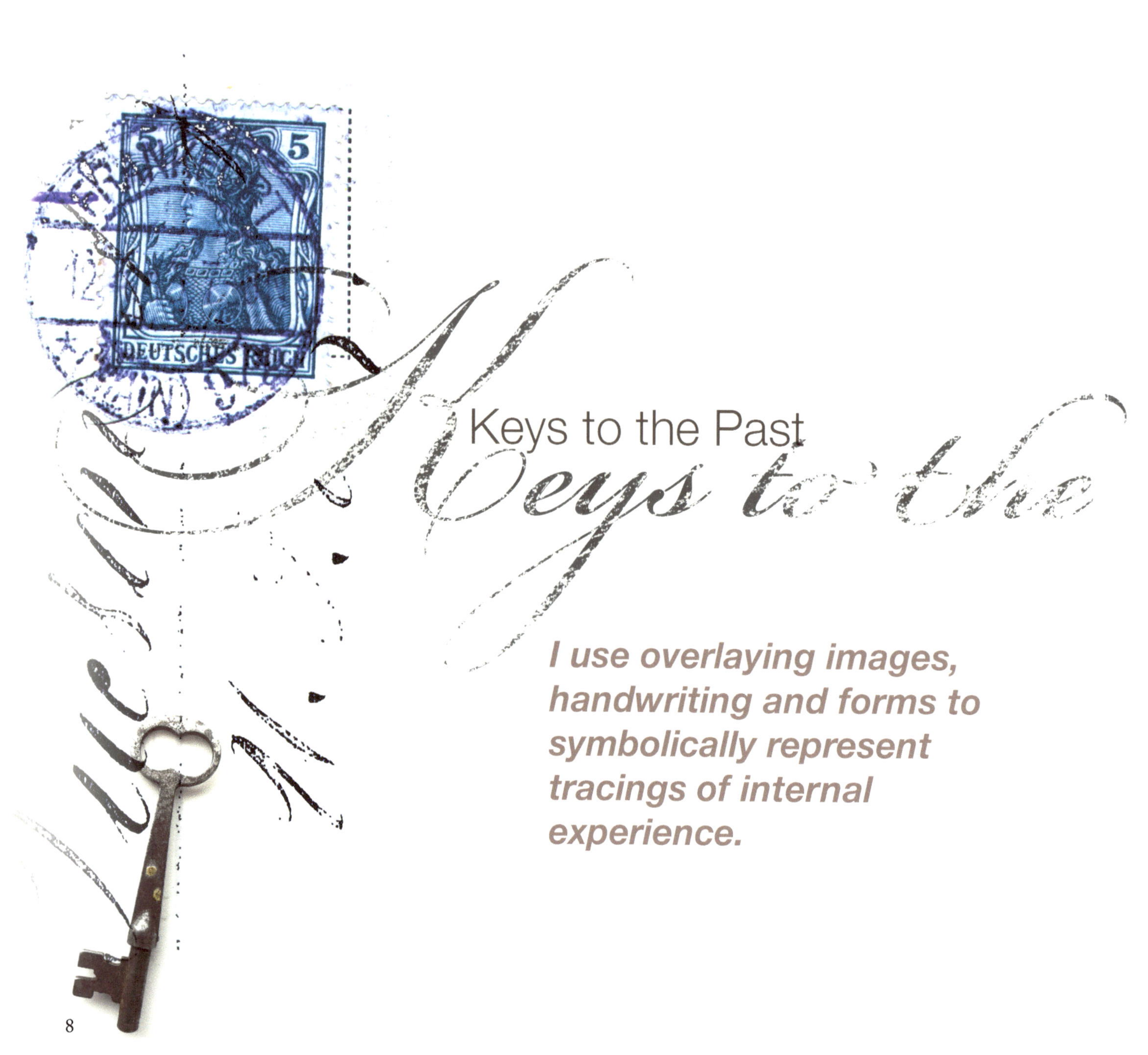

Keys to the Past

I use overlaying images, handwriting and forms to symbolically represent tracings of internal experience.

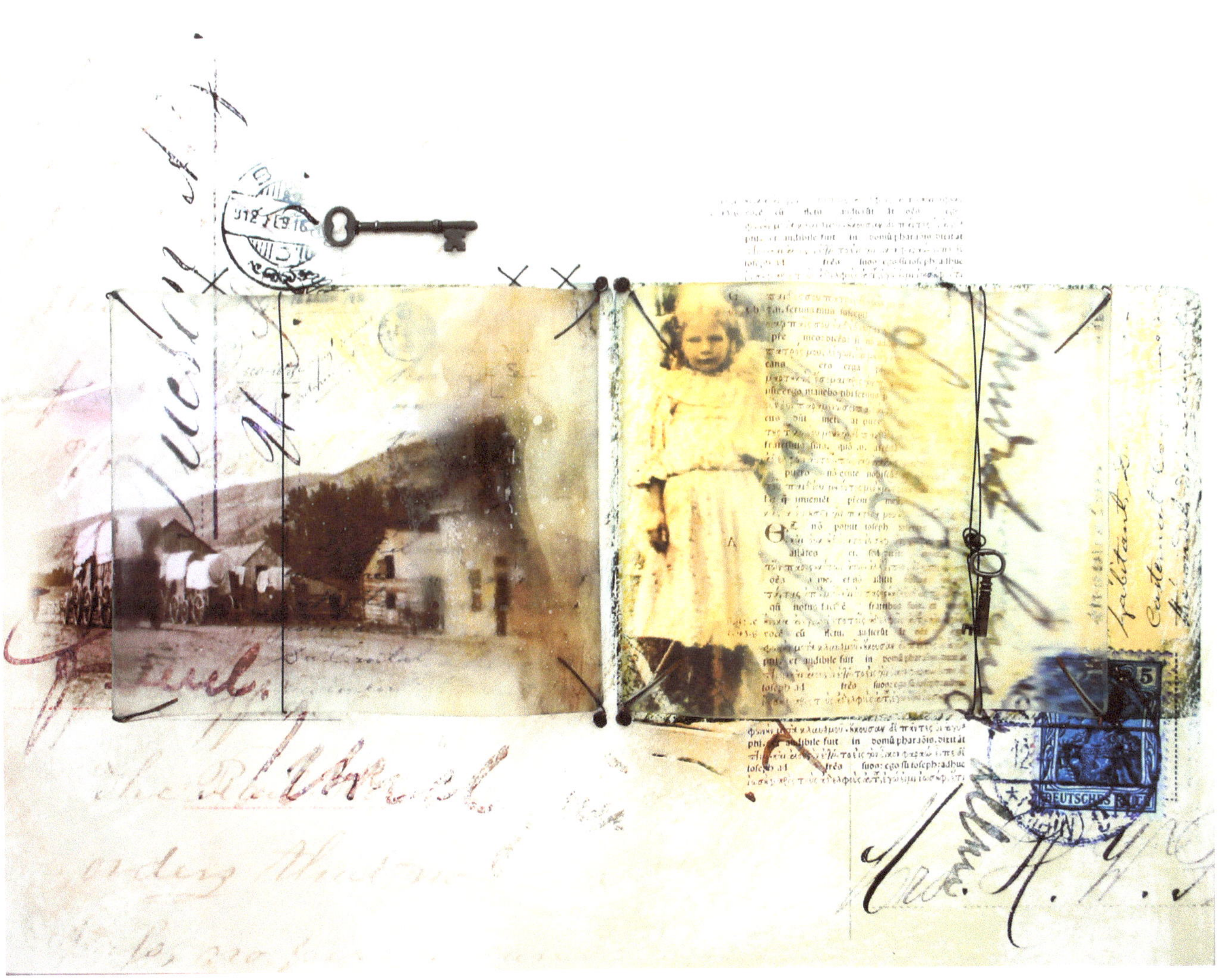

Past

Keys to the Past

Sandy Young

mixed media with kiln-formed glass,
antique keys, wire, tacks on birch panel
18" x 24" x 3" (2011)

Train Late

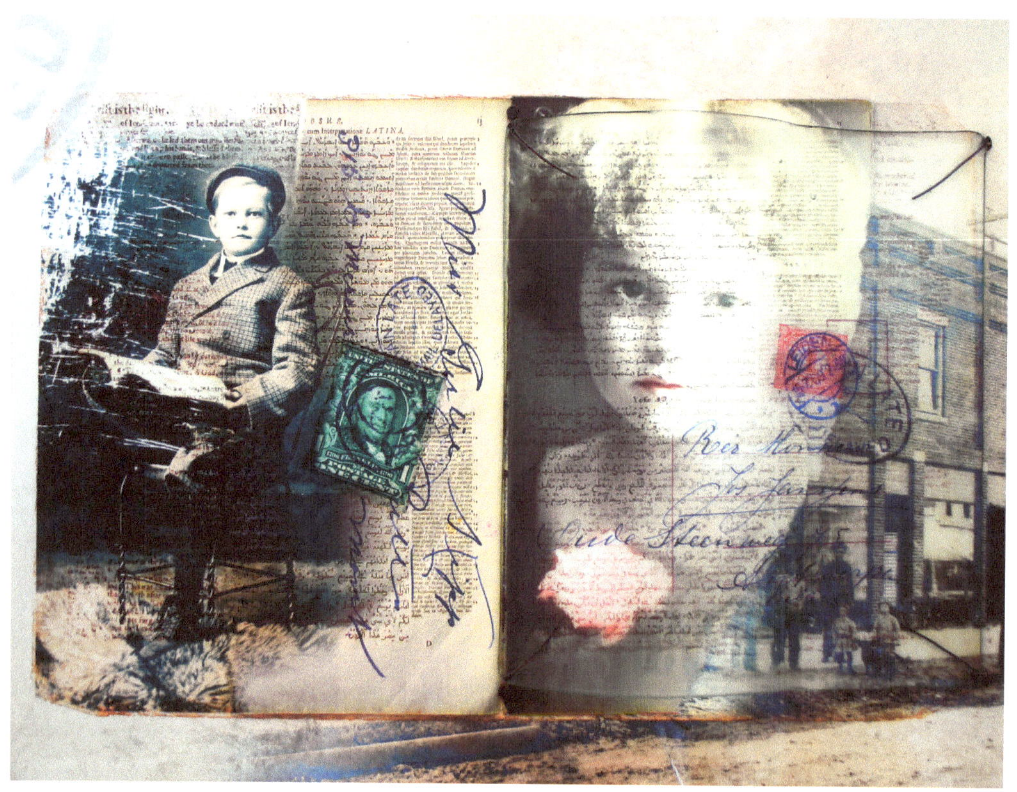

Mail Delayed
Sandy Young
mixed media with kiln-formed glass,
wire, tacks, on birch panel
18" x 24" x 3" (2012)

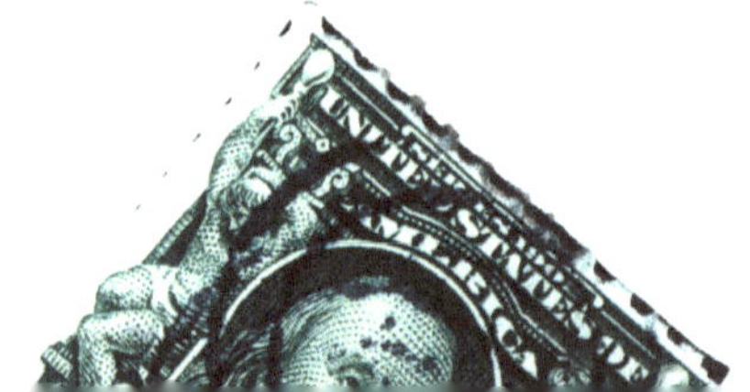

Mail delayed

***M**ail Delayed* was inspired by the stamped mark "Train Late, Mail Delayed" found on a 1906 letter. The mark, pictured right, is used twice in the artwork. The book form, with wavy kiln-formed glass overlay, suggests a story about the children pictured in the piece.

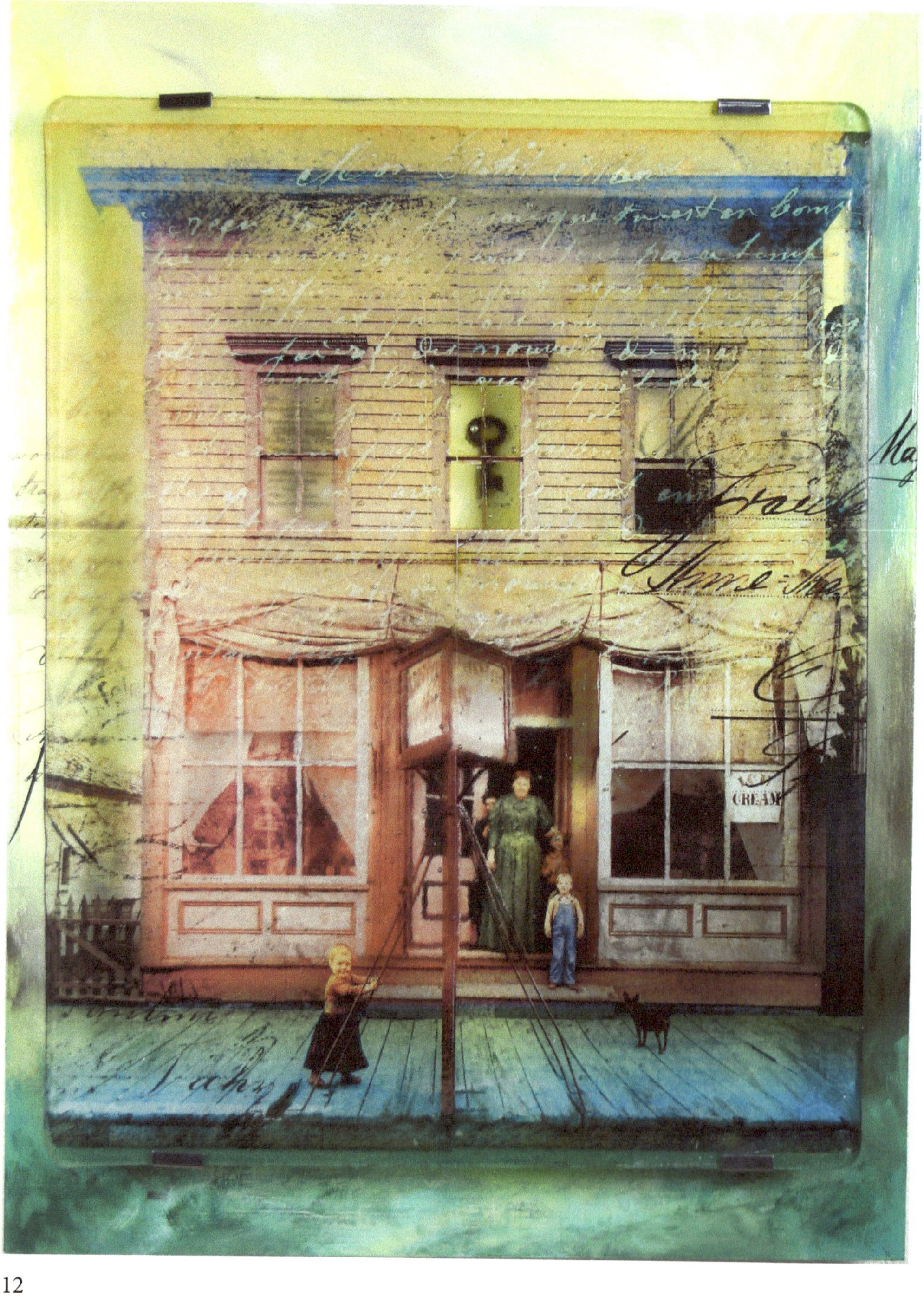

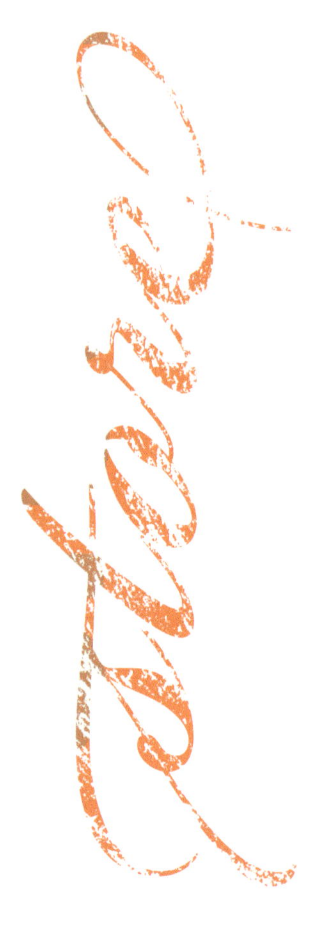

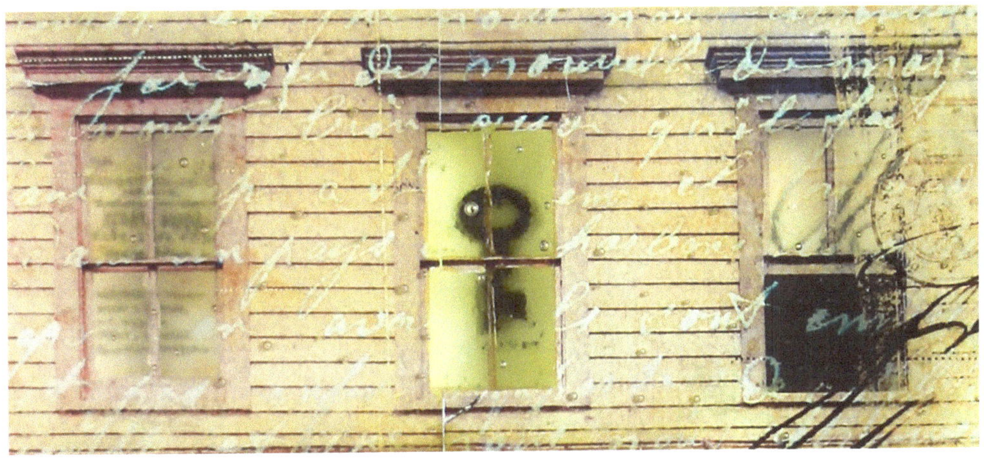

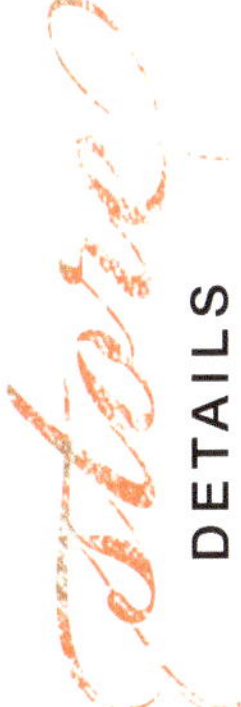

< Ice Cream Store

Sandy Young
mixed media with kiln-formed glass,
antique key, on birch panel
24" x 18" x 2" (2011)

The entrance area and windows in the artwork *Ice Cream Store* are translucent. An actual antique key and various writing can be seen through the windows. The boy in overalls, the little girl and dog are all on the glass plane while the other figures are behind the glass on the back panel, adding to the sense of depth.

Above: Detail of "Ice Cream Store" showing antique key and writing viewed through the upper glass windows.

Right: Detail of "Ice Cream Store". The family in the doorway is viewed through the glass. The boy in the overalls is repeated on the glass.

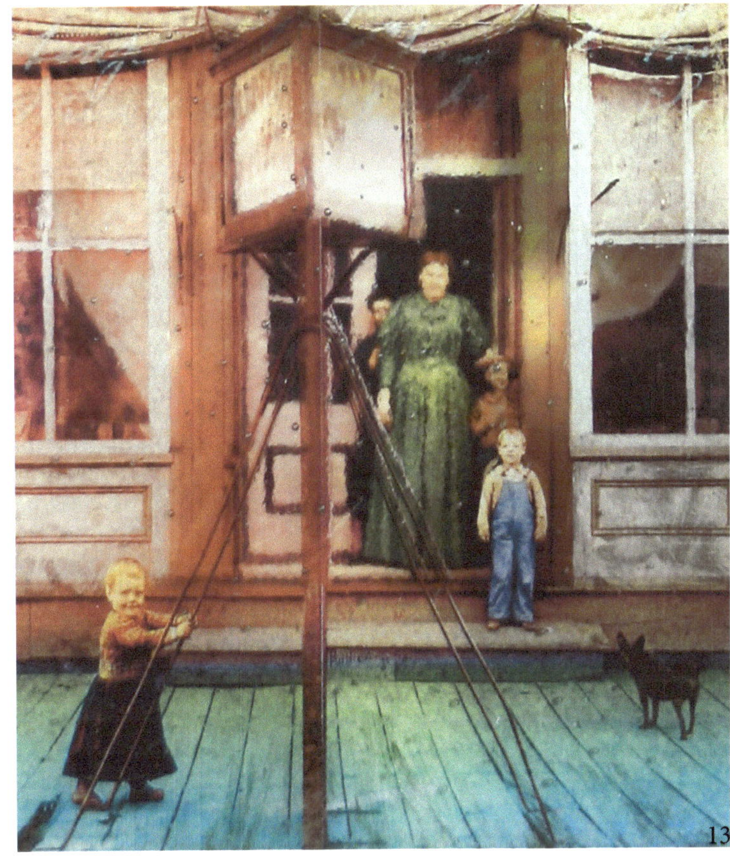

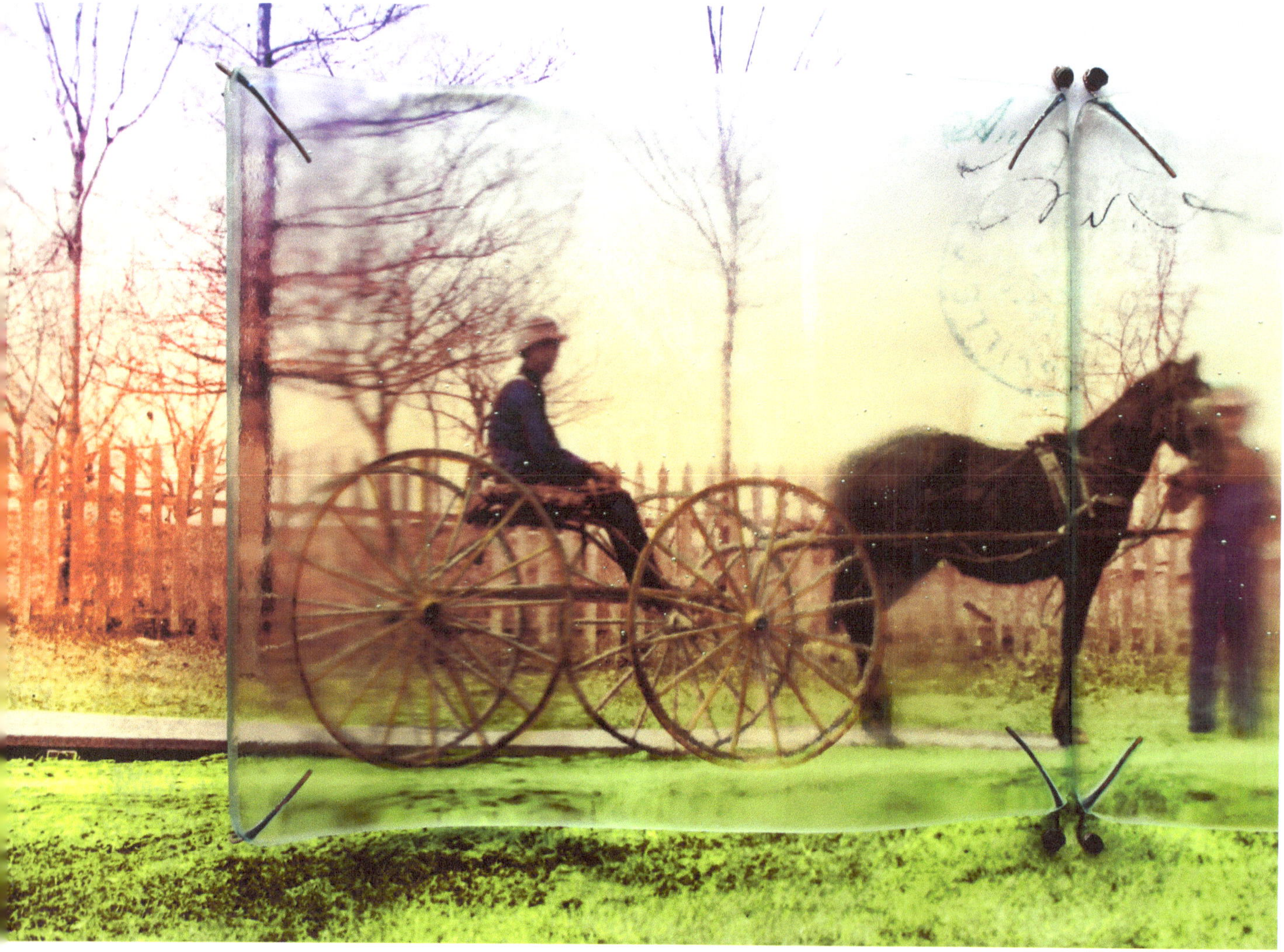

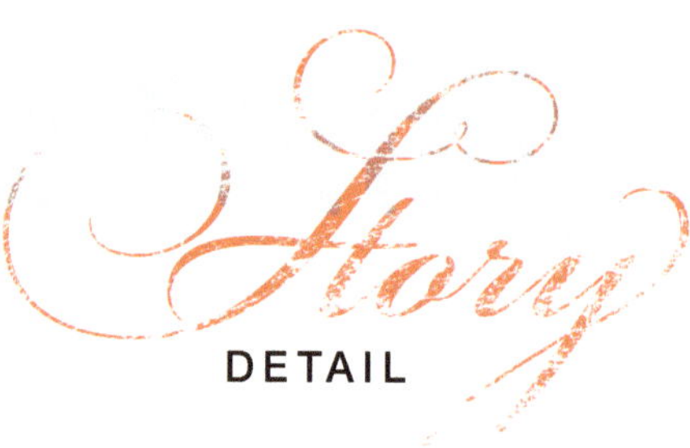

Above: Detail of "The Family Story". Wagon wheels are on both the glass and background panel. The experience of depth changes with viewing angle.

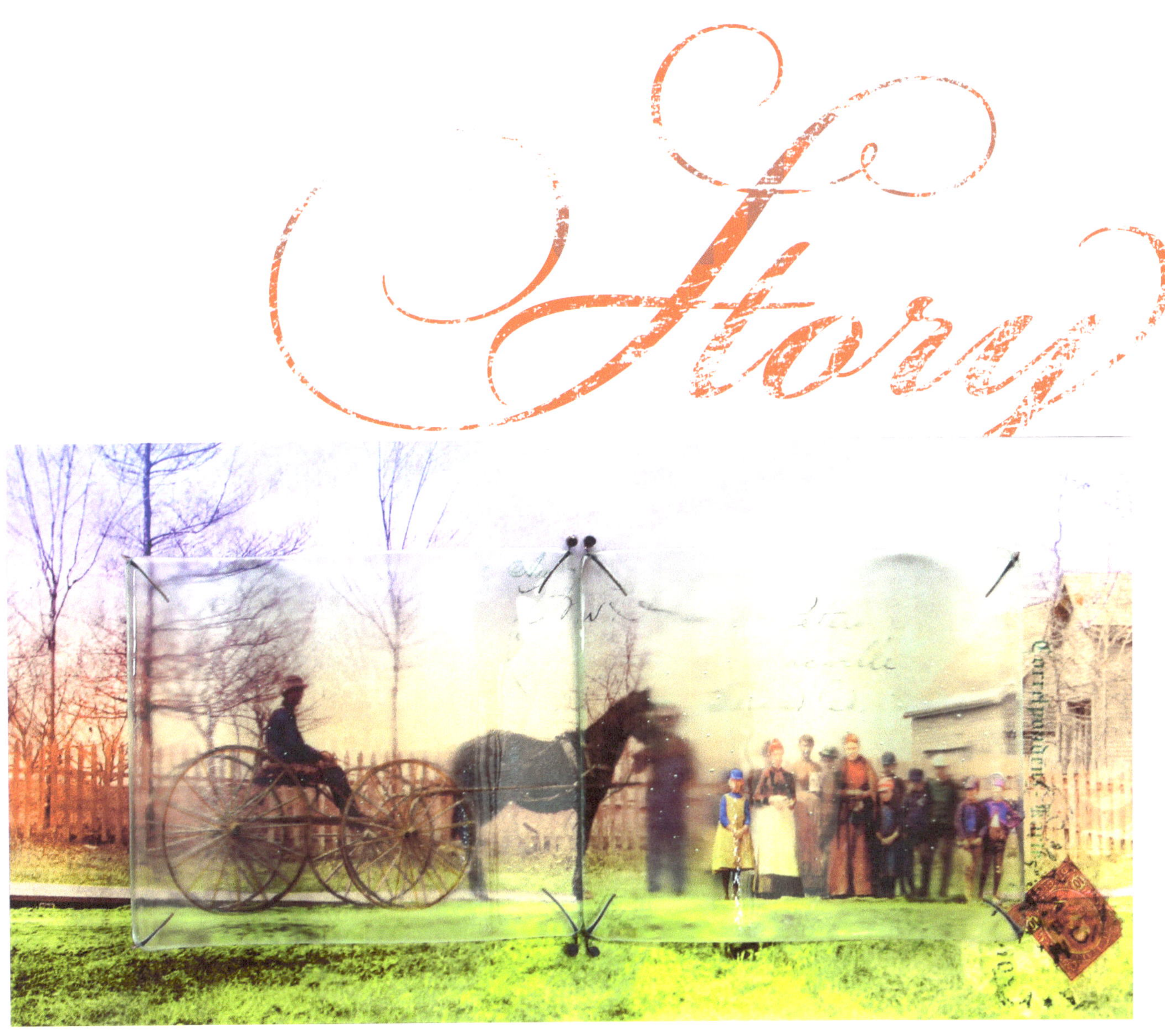

The Family Story
Sandy Young
mixed media with kiln-formed glass, wire, tacks, on birch panel
12" x 24" x 3" (2012)

In this photograph of *The Family Story,* reflections on the glass give a sense of the dimensional nature of the artwork. Some of the figures are painted on the glass while others are on the back panel, adding to the 3-dimensional effect.

Halbrite Drug Store

drug store

Halbrite Drug Store

Sandy Young
mixed media with kiln-formed glass,
wire, tacks, on birch panel
30" x 40" x 2" (2012)

The distressed building facade of *Halbrite Drug Store* has areas of transparency where writing from the background panel shows through. The windows are translucent allowing a view into the store interior. A young boy is seen standing in the doorway, behind the clear glass at the door.

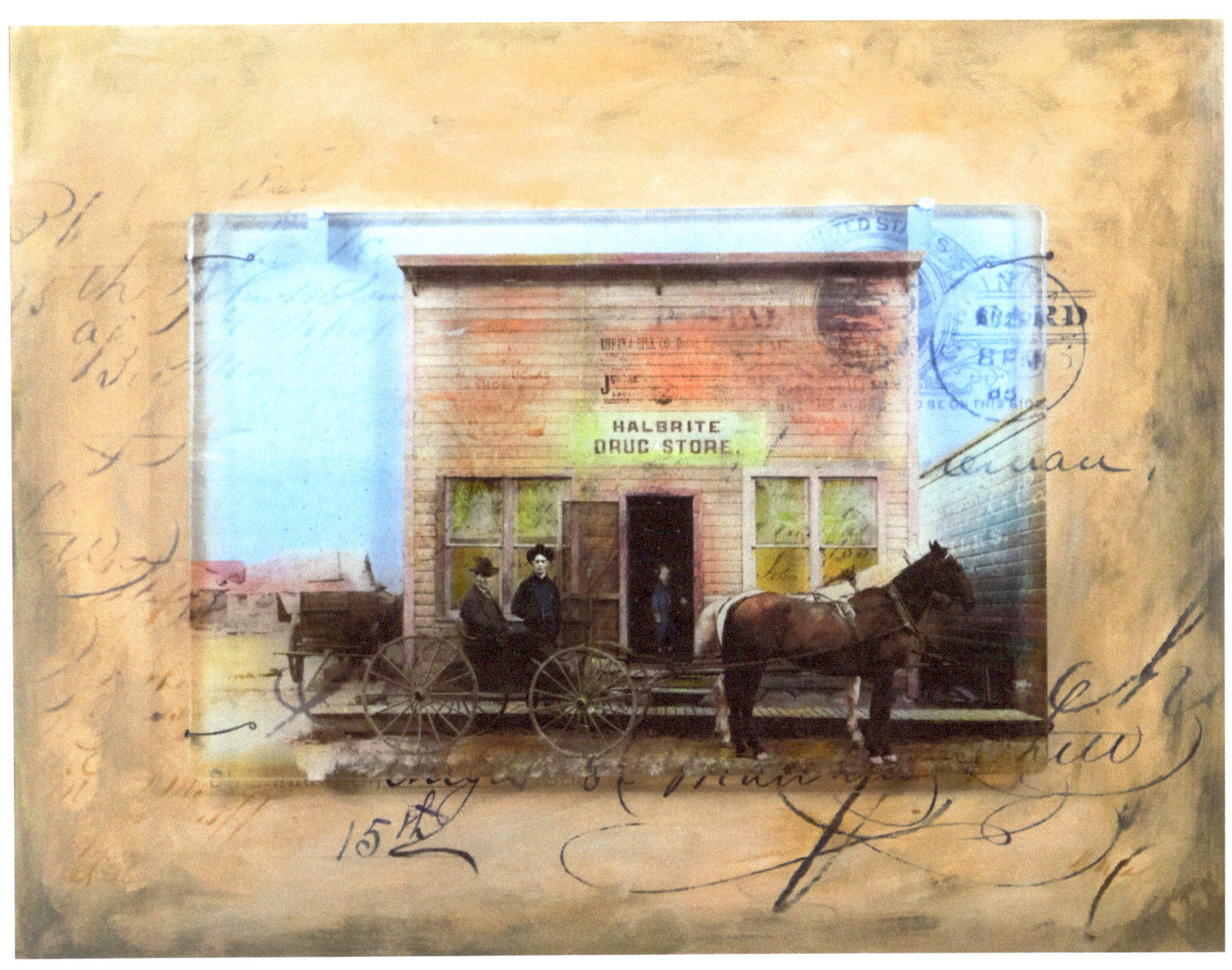
HALBRITE
DRUG STORE.

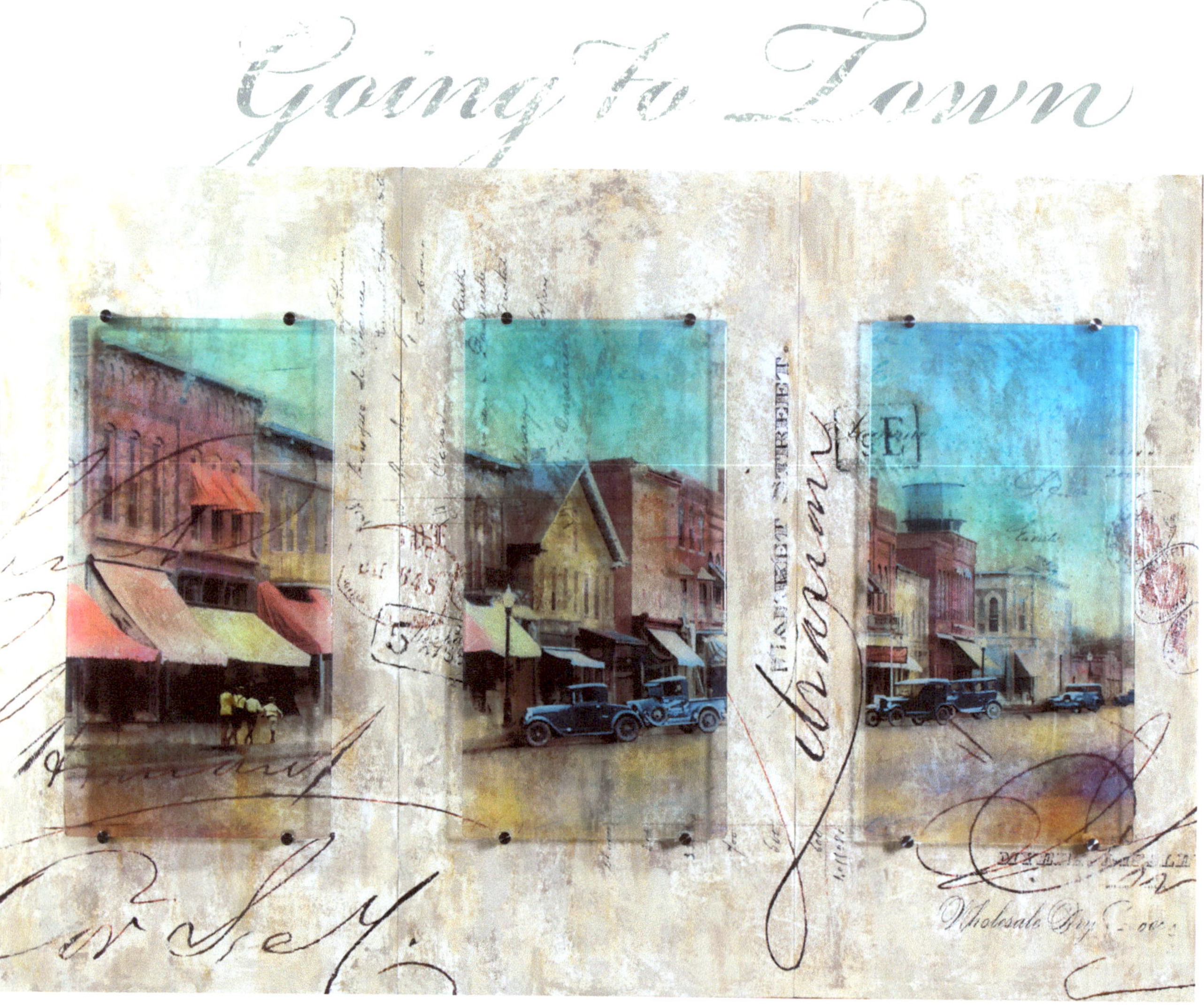

Going to Town

Sandy Young

mixed media with kiln-formed glass on birch panel

48" x 72" x 2.5" (2013)

Right: Detail of "Going to Town".

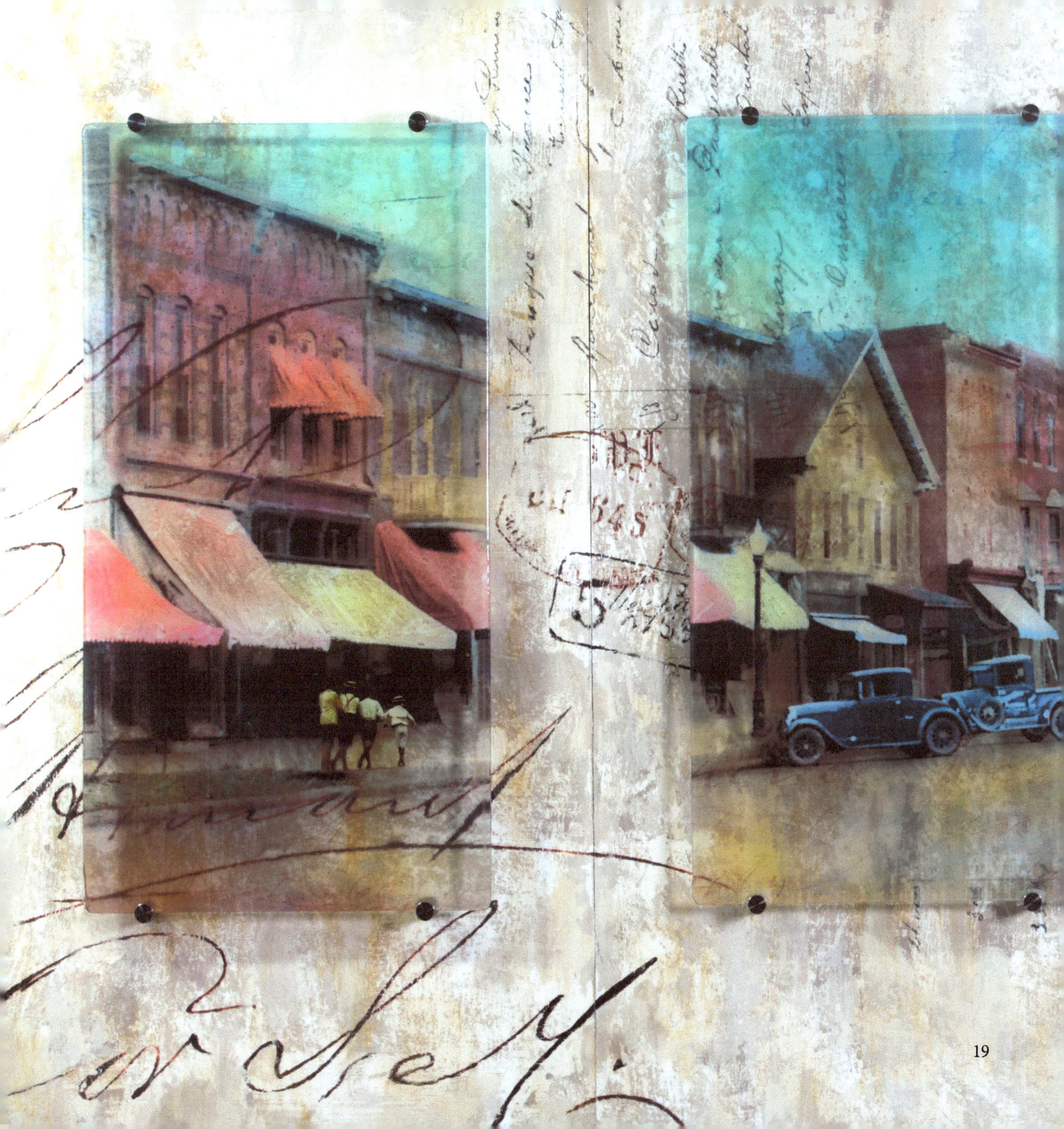

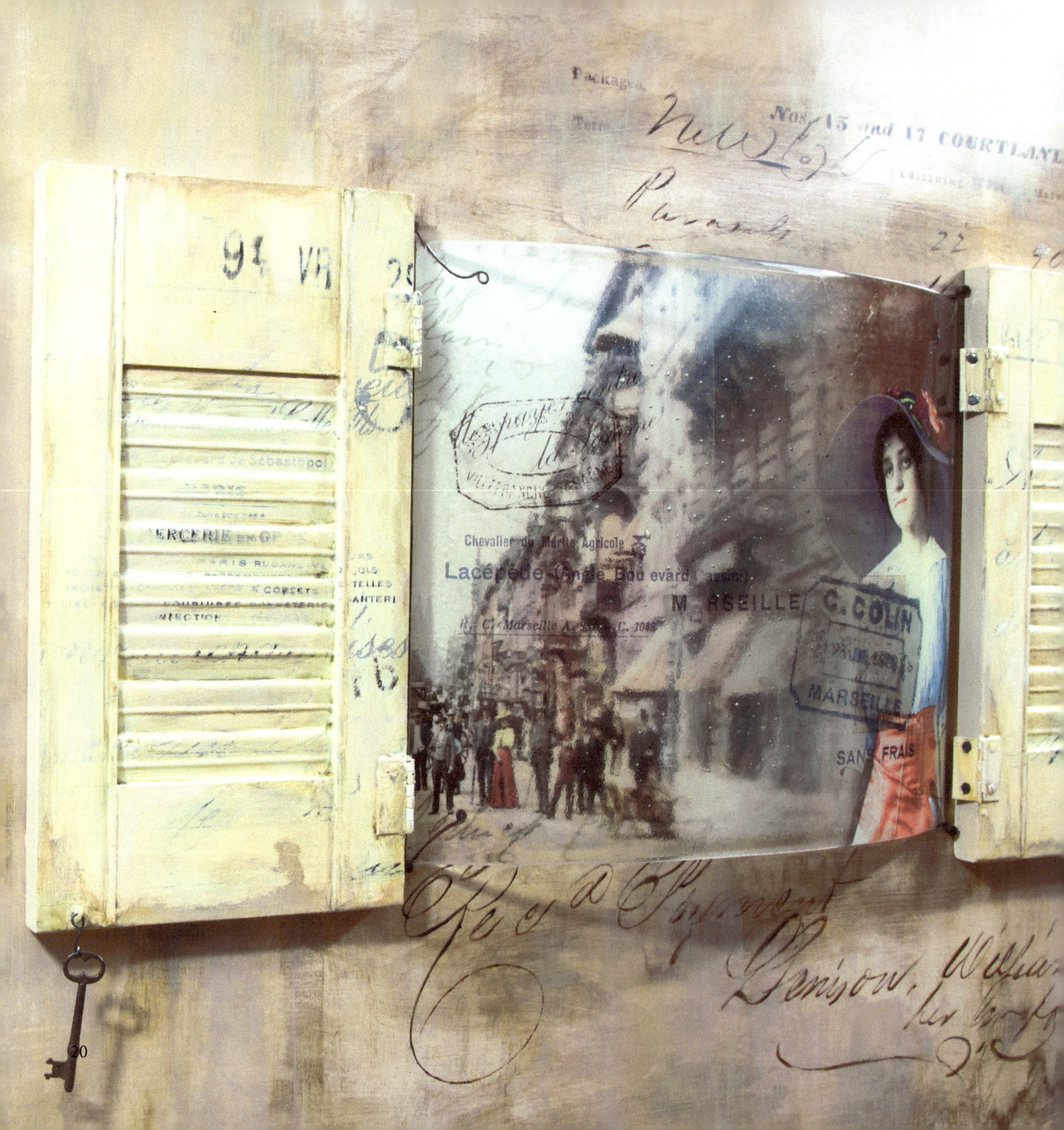
Packages
Nos 15 and 17 COURTLAND
94 VR
Chevalier du Mérite Agricole
MARSEILLE
C. COLIN
MARSEILLE
SANS FRAIS
ERCERIE EN GROS

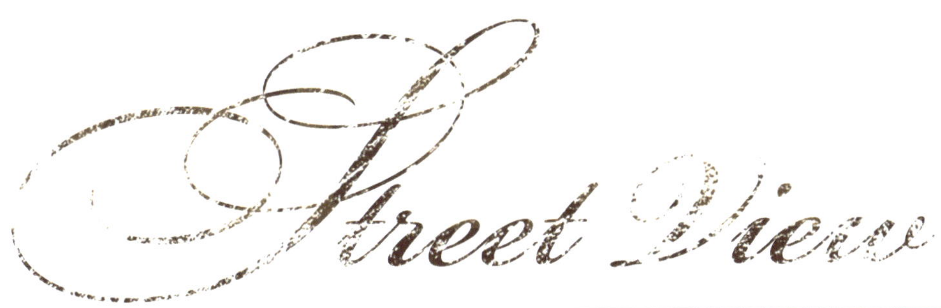

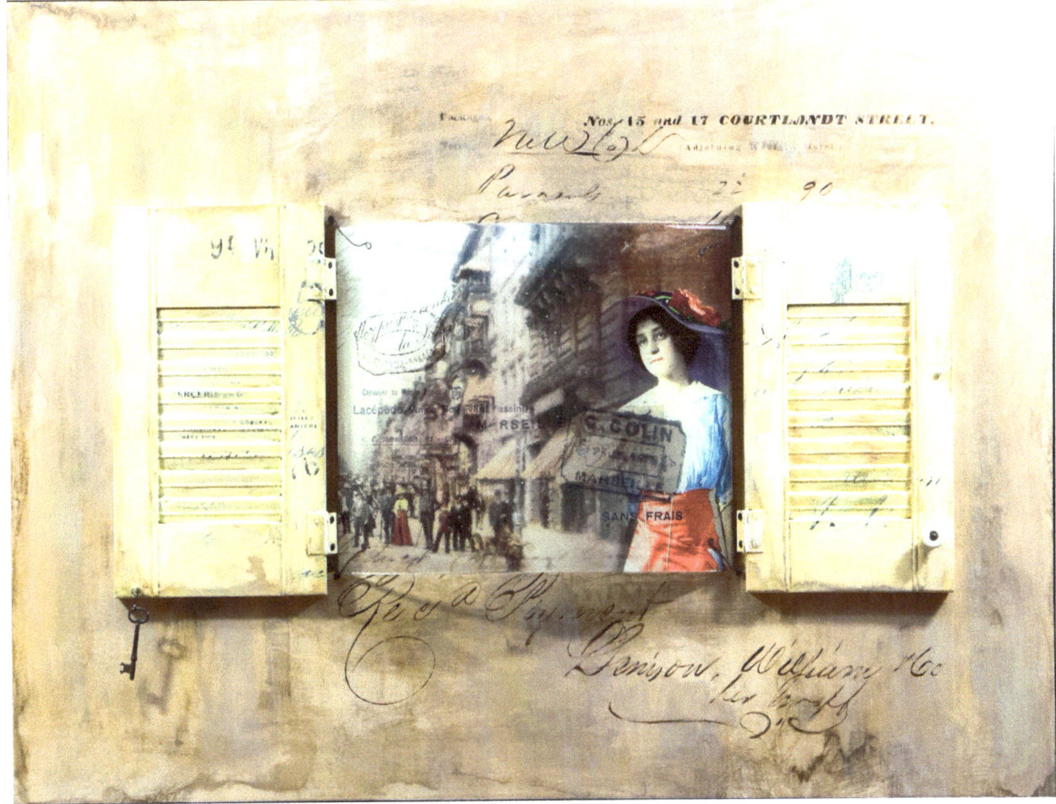

In *Street View*, altered vintage shutters frame curved kiln-formed glass creating a window to the street outside. Imagery on both the glass and back panel combine to create a 3-dimensional scene.

Left: Detail of "Street View" at an angle showing the curvature of the kiln-formed glass.

Street View

Sandy Young

mixed media with kiln-formed glass, shutters, antique key, wire, tacks, on birch panel

30" x 40" x 4" (2012)

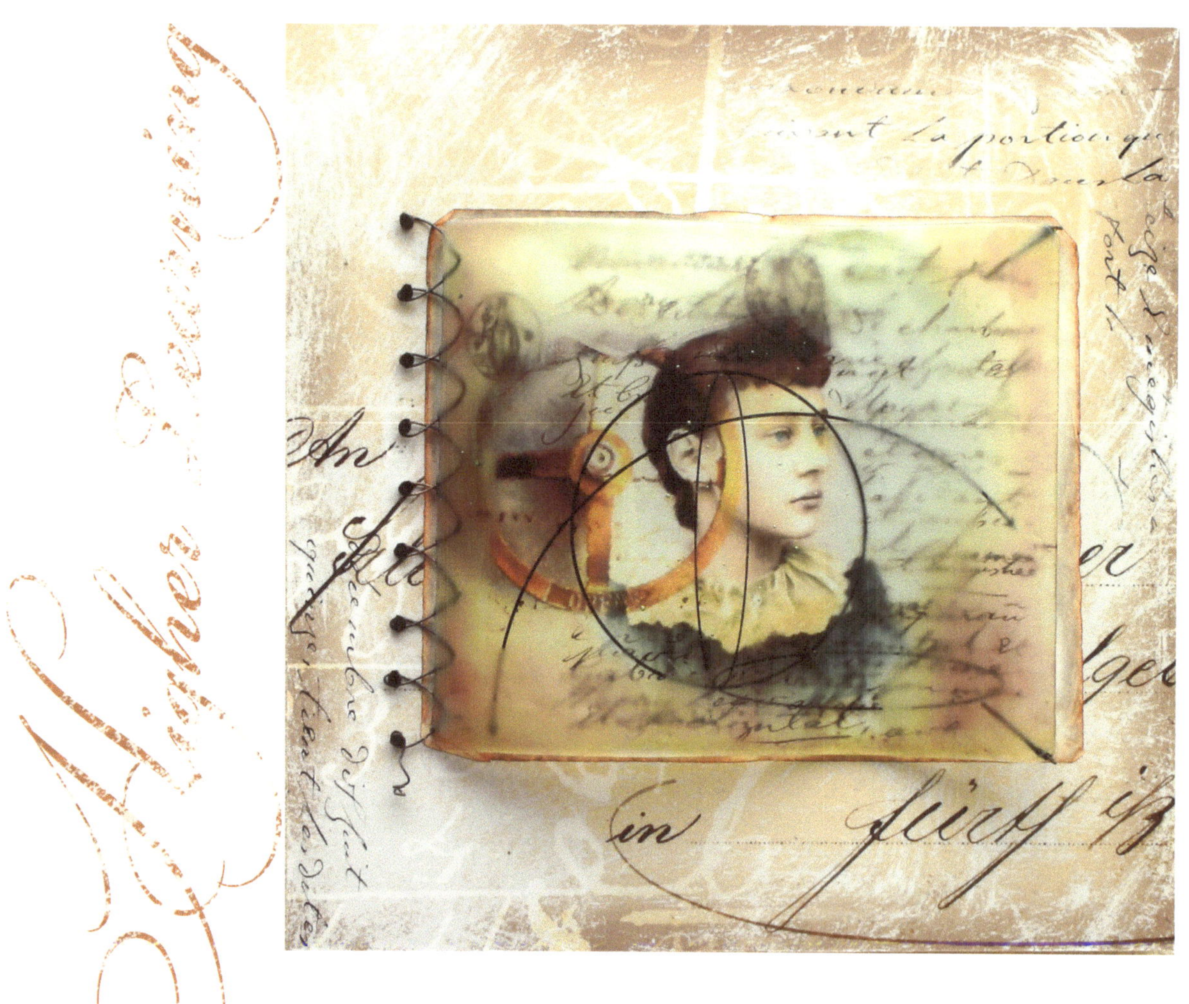

^ **Higher Learning**

Sandy Young

mixed media with kiln-formed glass, encaustic, wire, tacks, on birch panel

14" x 14" x 2" (2012)

> **Passages**

Sandy Young

mixed media with kiln-formed glass, wire, tacks, on birch panel

18.5" x 18.5" x 2.5" (2012)

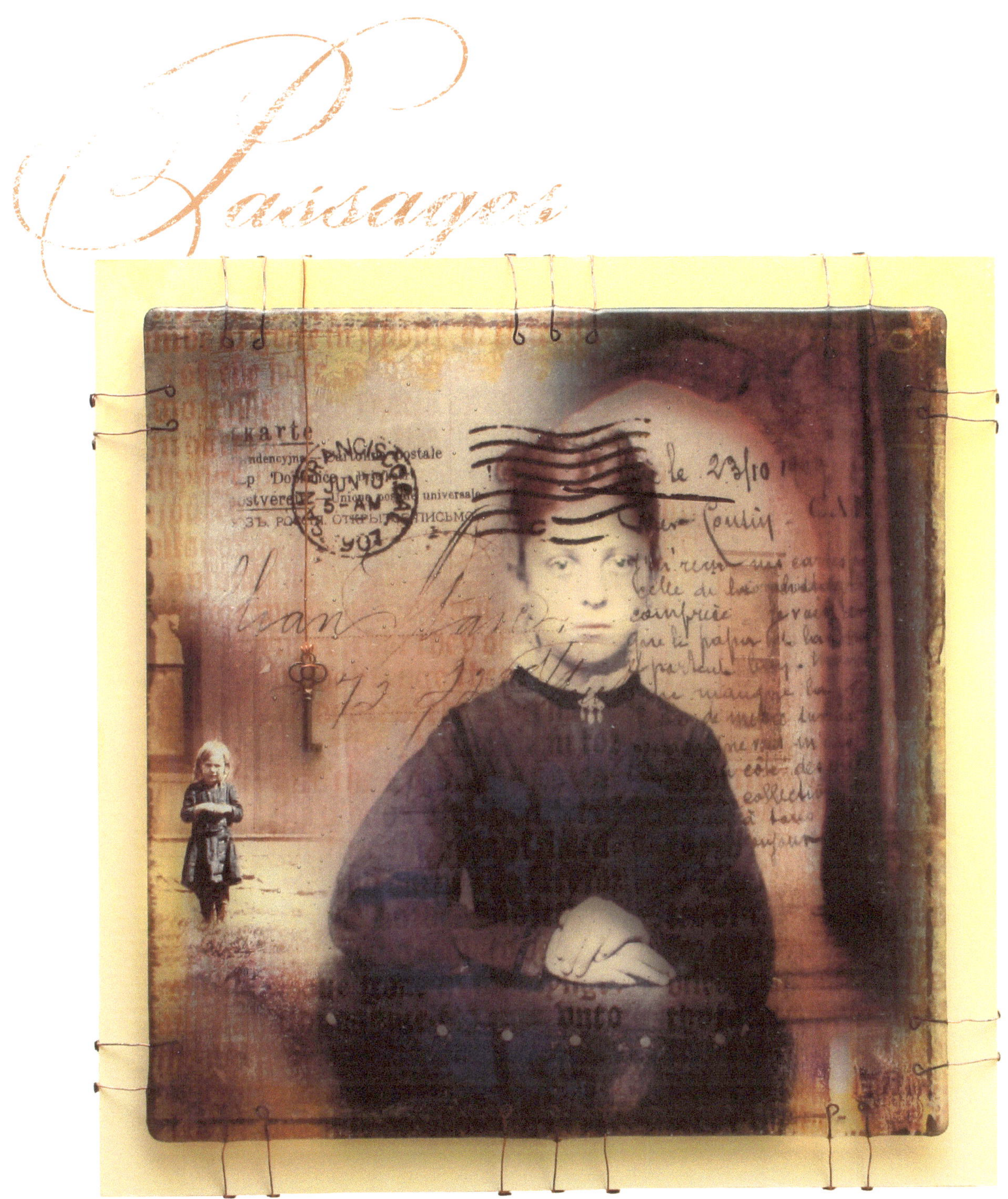
Paisages
karte
postale
universale
le 23/10

Artwork Inspired by...

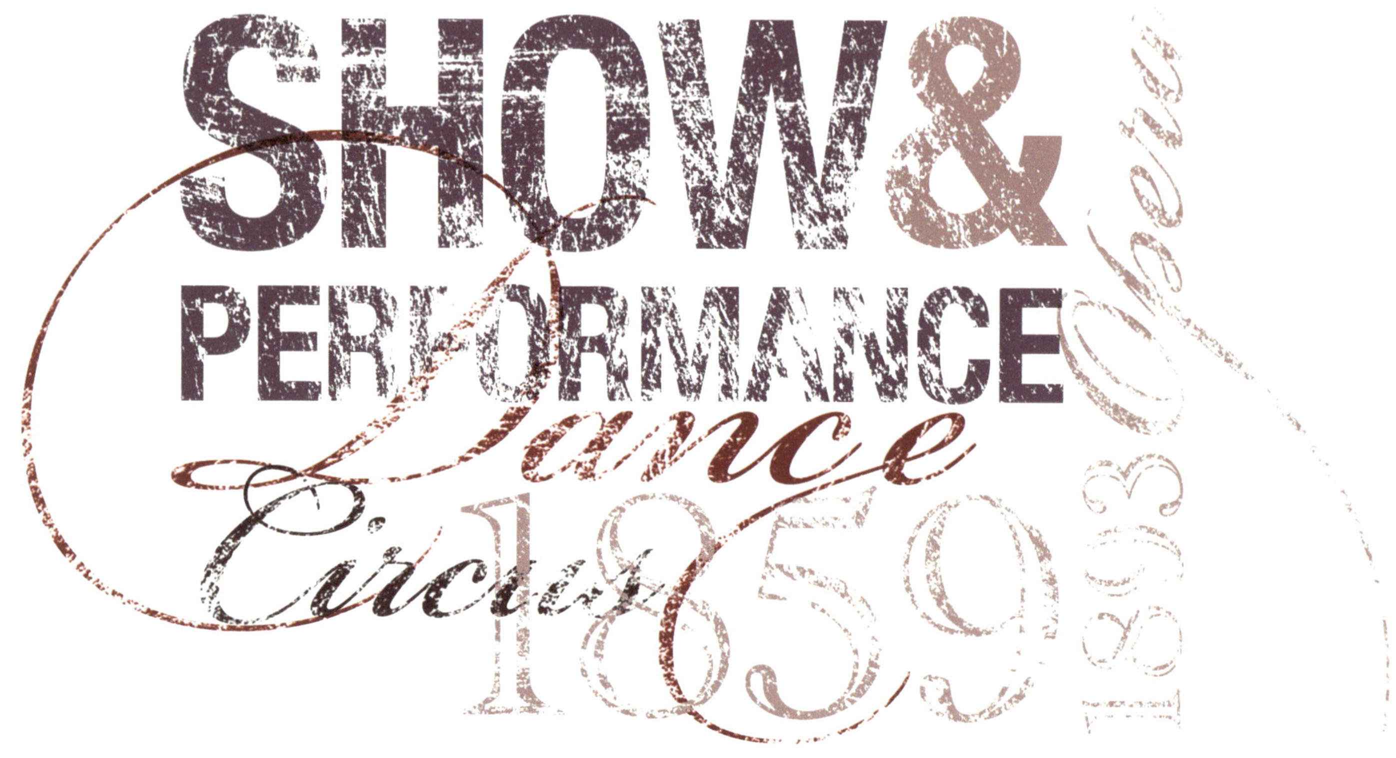

The next several pages highlight some of the artwork that was inspired by show posters of the 1800's and early 1900's. In mixing old with new, I often juxtapose contemporary figures with old time-worn show posters, in imaginary settings.

In *Cirque*, contemporary dancers preparing for a performance are viewed through a glass doorway of a building where old, oversized circus posters line the wall.

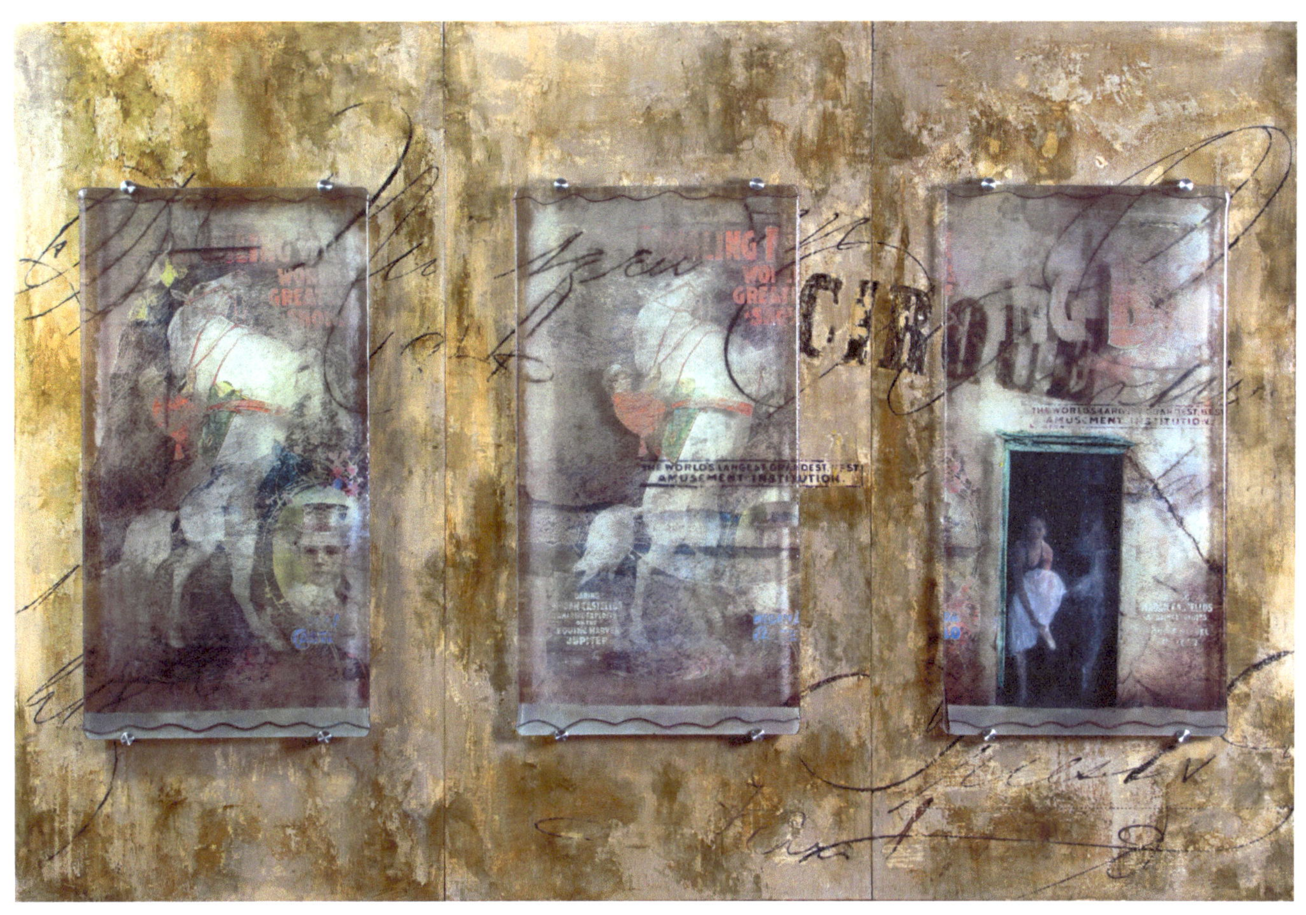

Cirque

Sandy Young
mixed media with kiln-formed glass
on birch panel
48" x 72" x 2.5" (2013)

Next page spread: Detail of "Cirque". >

CIRQUE

Cirque

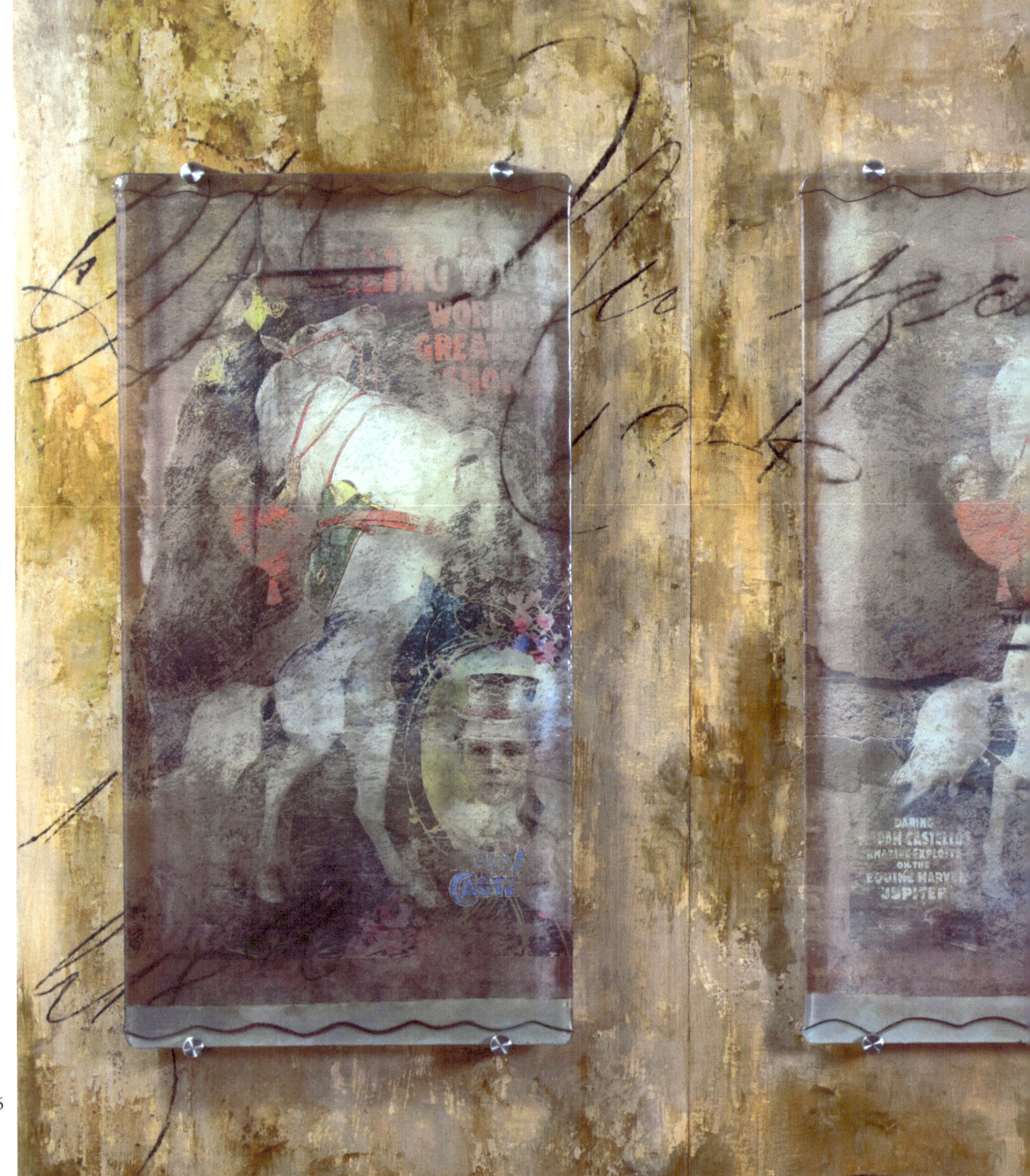
DARING
ON THE
JUPITER

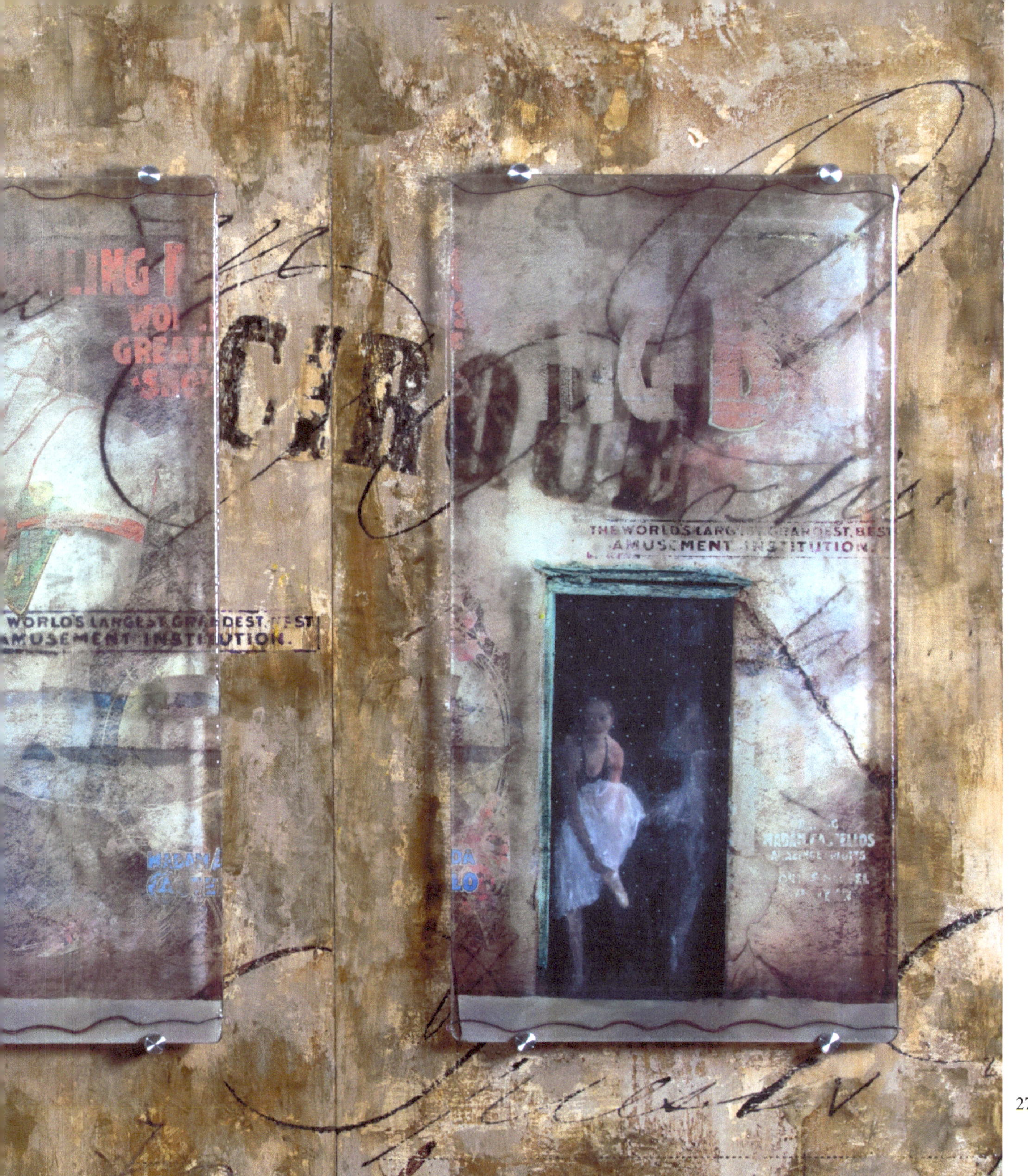
WORLD'S LARGEST GRANDEST BEST
AMUSEMENT INSTITUTION.
AMUSEMENT INSTITUTION.

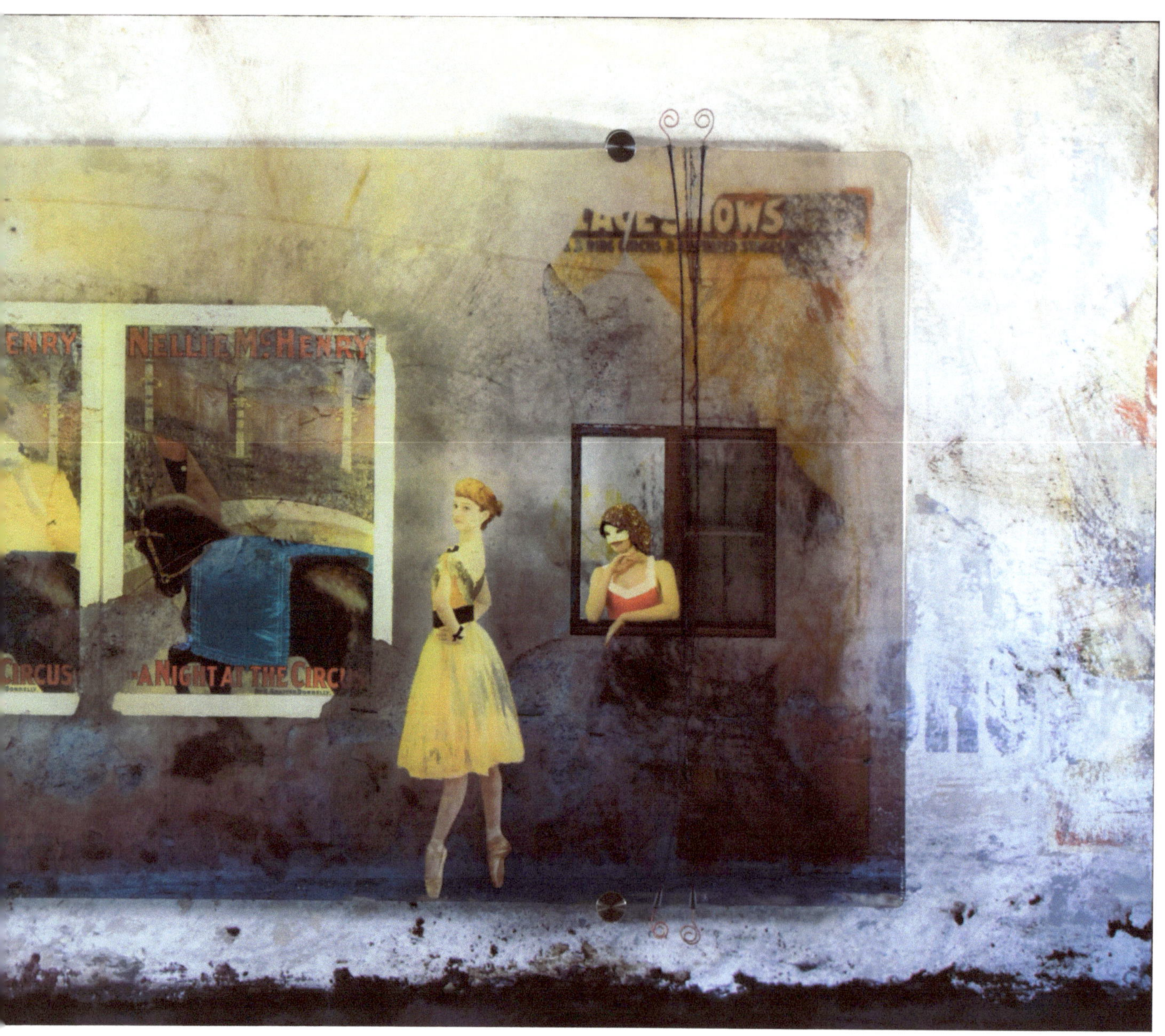
HENRY
CIRCUS
NELLIE McHENRY
A NIGHT AT THE CIRC

Night After The Circus

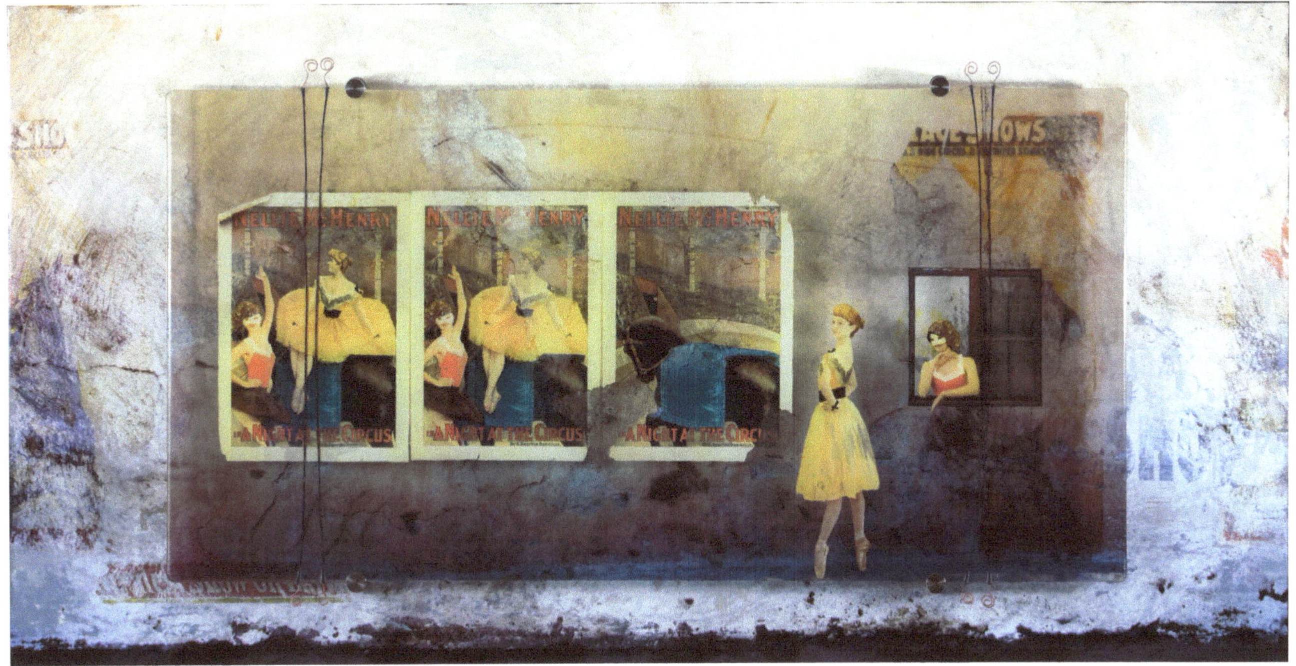

Night After the Circus

Sandy Young
mixed media with kiln-formed glass, wire, on birch panel
24" x 48" x 3" (2014)

Left: Detail of "Night After the Circus".

The idea behind *Night After the Circus* is that old circus posters come to life at night after the circus is over. The art shows three antique circus posters plastered to a distressed building facade. To the right of the third poster are the characters from the poster who, apparently, have jumped out of the poster frame and have come to life.

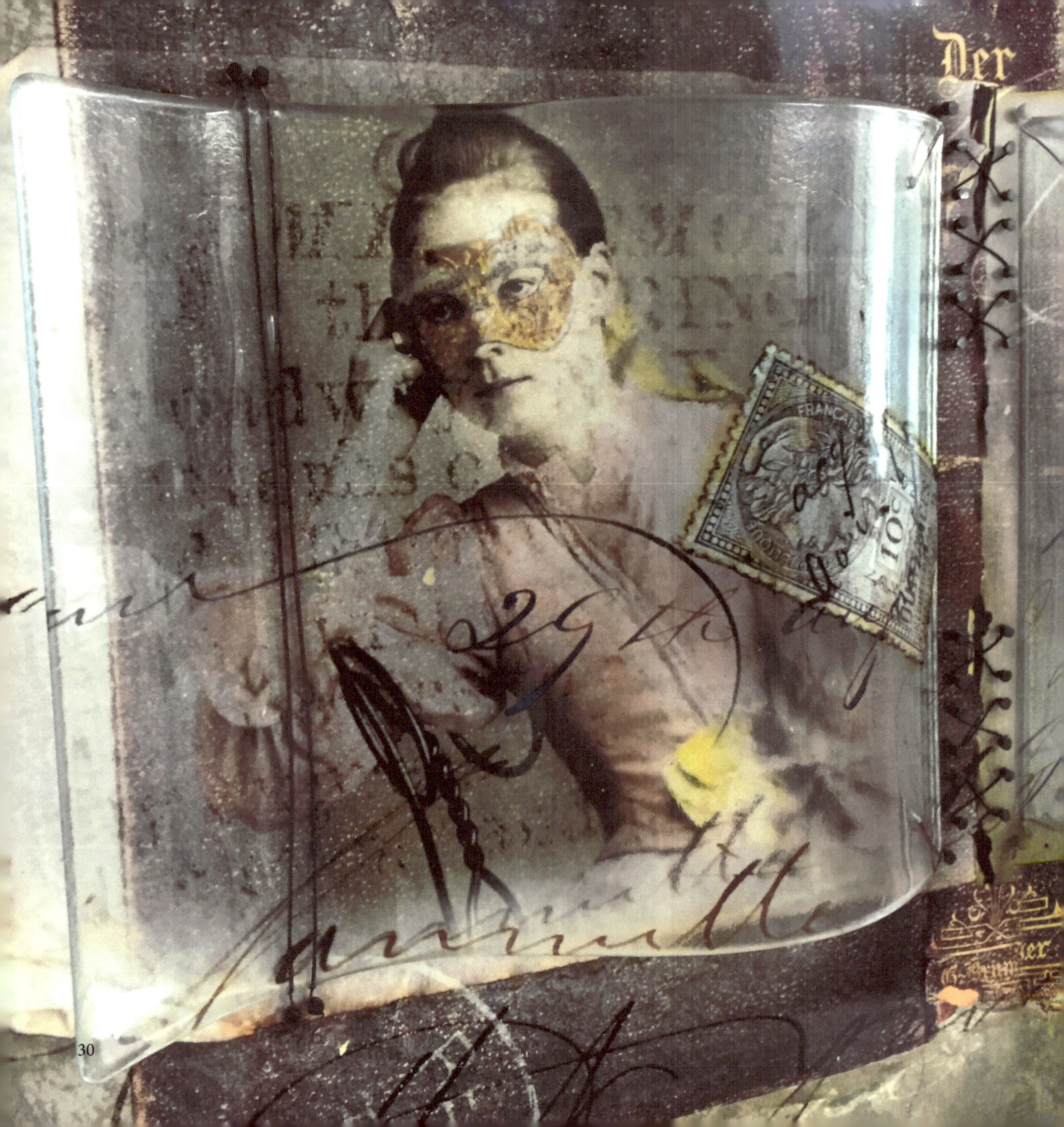
Der
FRANCAISE
10c

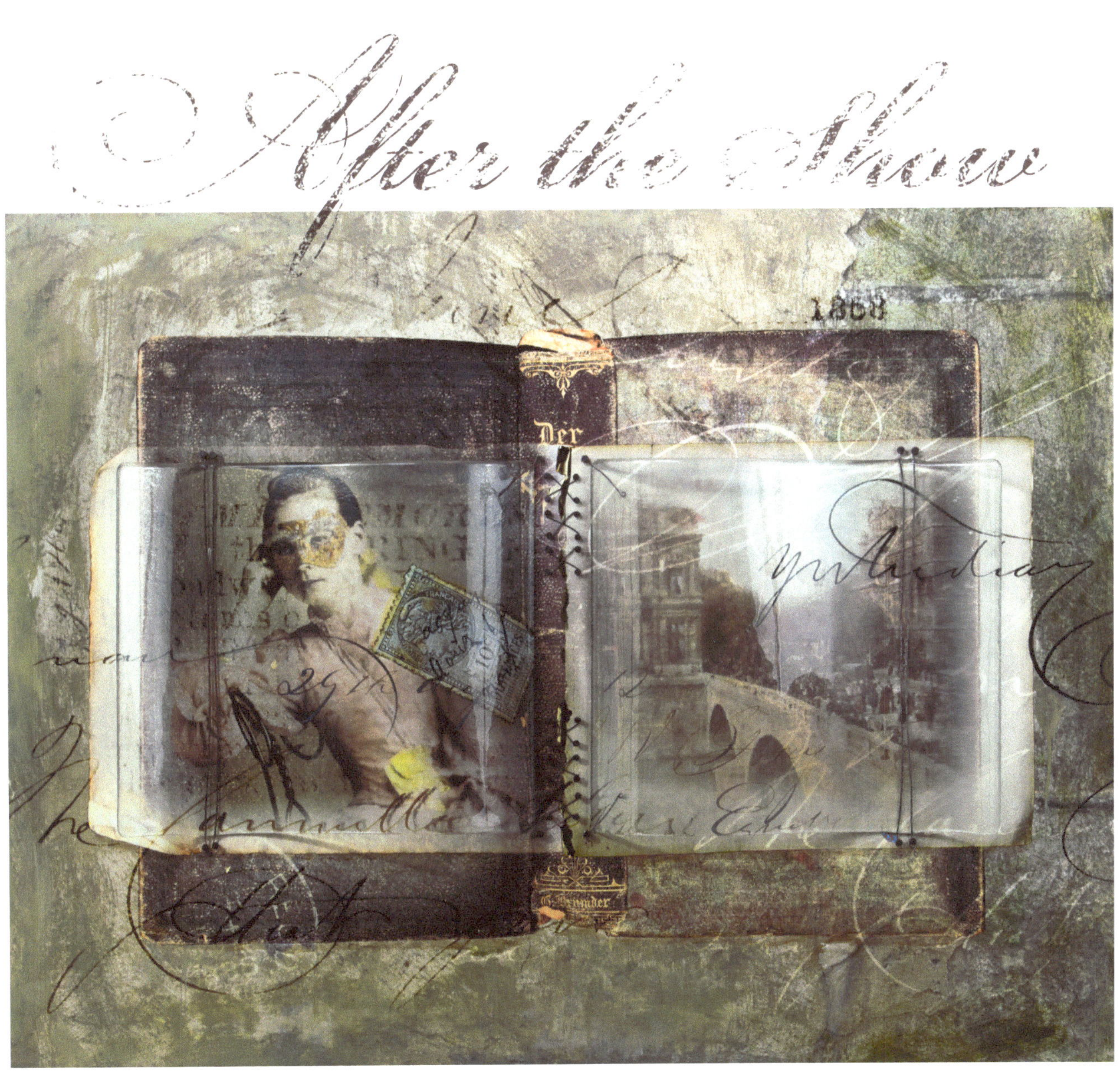

Left: Detail of "After the Show" at an angle showing the curvature of the kiln-formed glass.

After the Show

Sandy Young

mixed media with kiln-formed glass, wire, tacks, on birch panel

30" x 40" x 3" (2013)

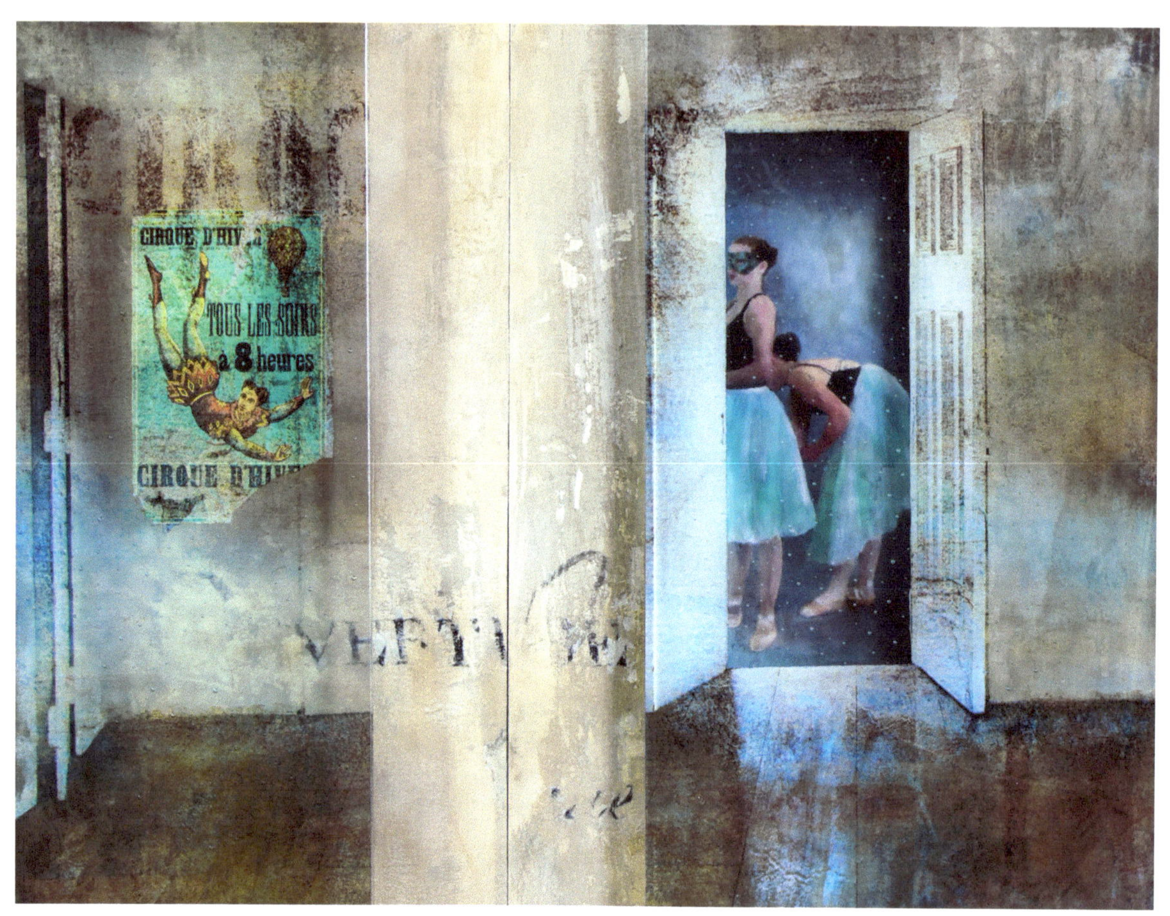

Dress Rehearsal

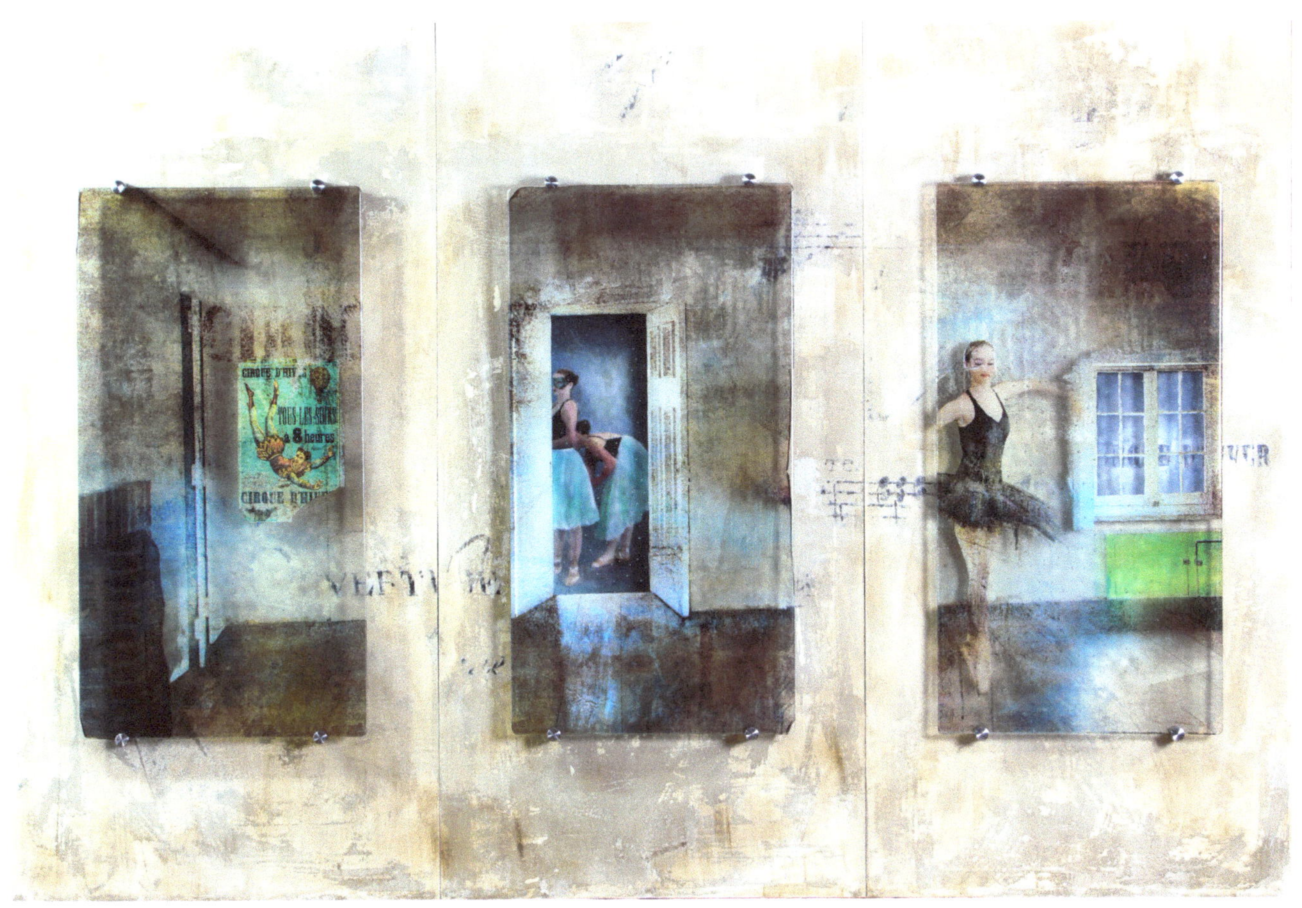

Dress Rehearsal

Sandy Young
mixed media with kiln-formed glass on birch panel
48” x 72” x 2.5” (2013)

Left: Detail of “Dress Rehearsal”.

D*ress Rehearsal* combines old with new. The ballet dancers are rehearsing in an old building where an 1800’s circus poster still hangs. The dancers in the doorway are behind the glass, on the base panel, while the image of the third ballerina is on the glass plane.

Aladdin's Lamp

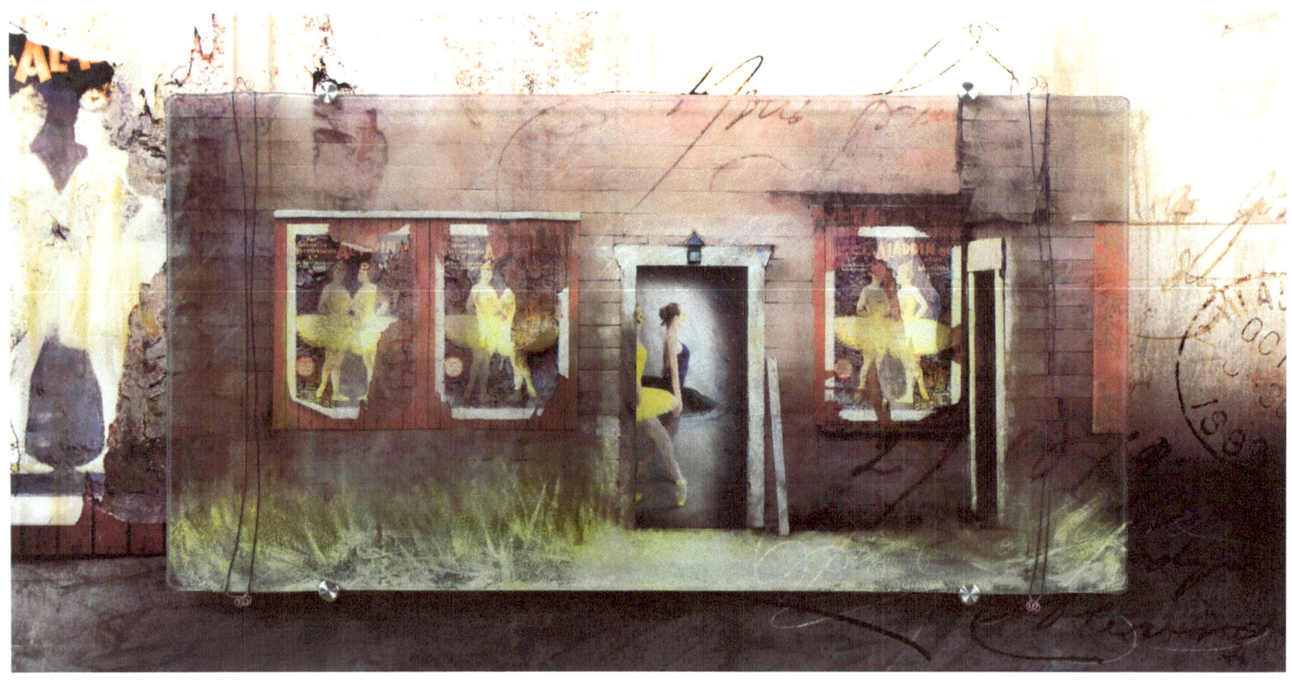

Aladdin's Lamp
Sandy Young
mixed media with kiln-formed glass, wire, on birch panel
48" x 24" x 2.5" (2013)

Similar to *Dress Rehearsal*, *Aladdin's Lamp* juxtaposes imagery from two different time periods. Here, we see a similarity between the contemporary ballet dancers in the doorway and the dancers depicted in the 1894 Aladdin show posters adorning the building.

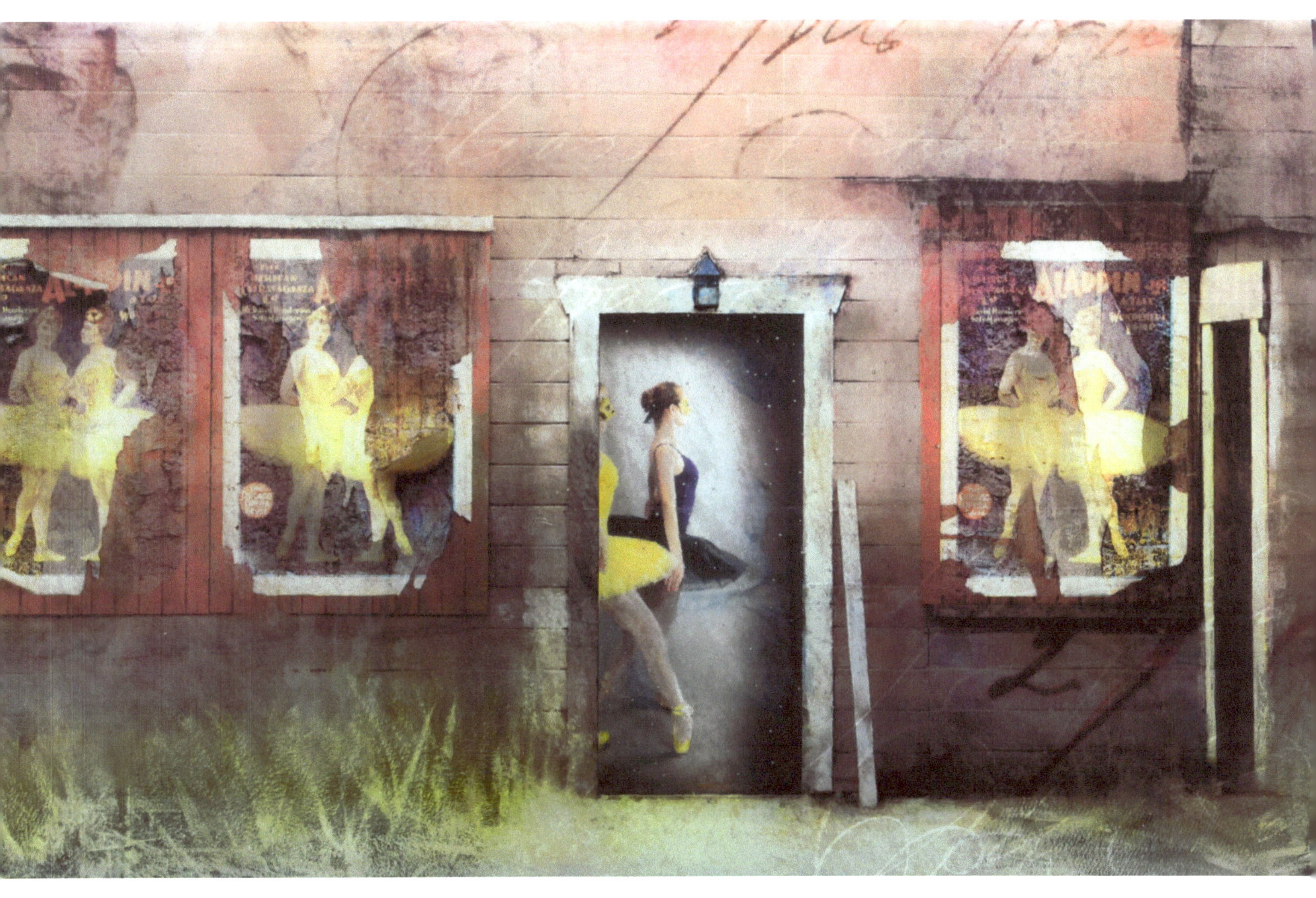

Above: Detail of "Aladdin's Lamp" glass panel. Dancers in the doorway are viewed through the glass. Varying levels of opacity in the glass panel allow portions of the background to show through.

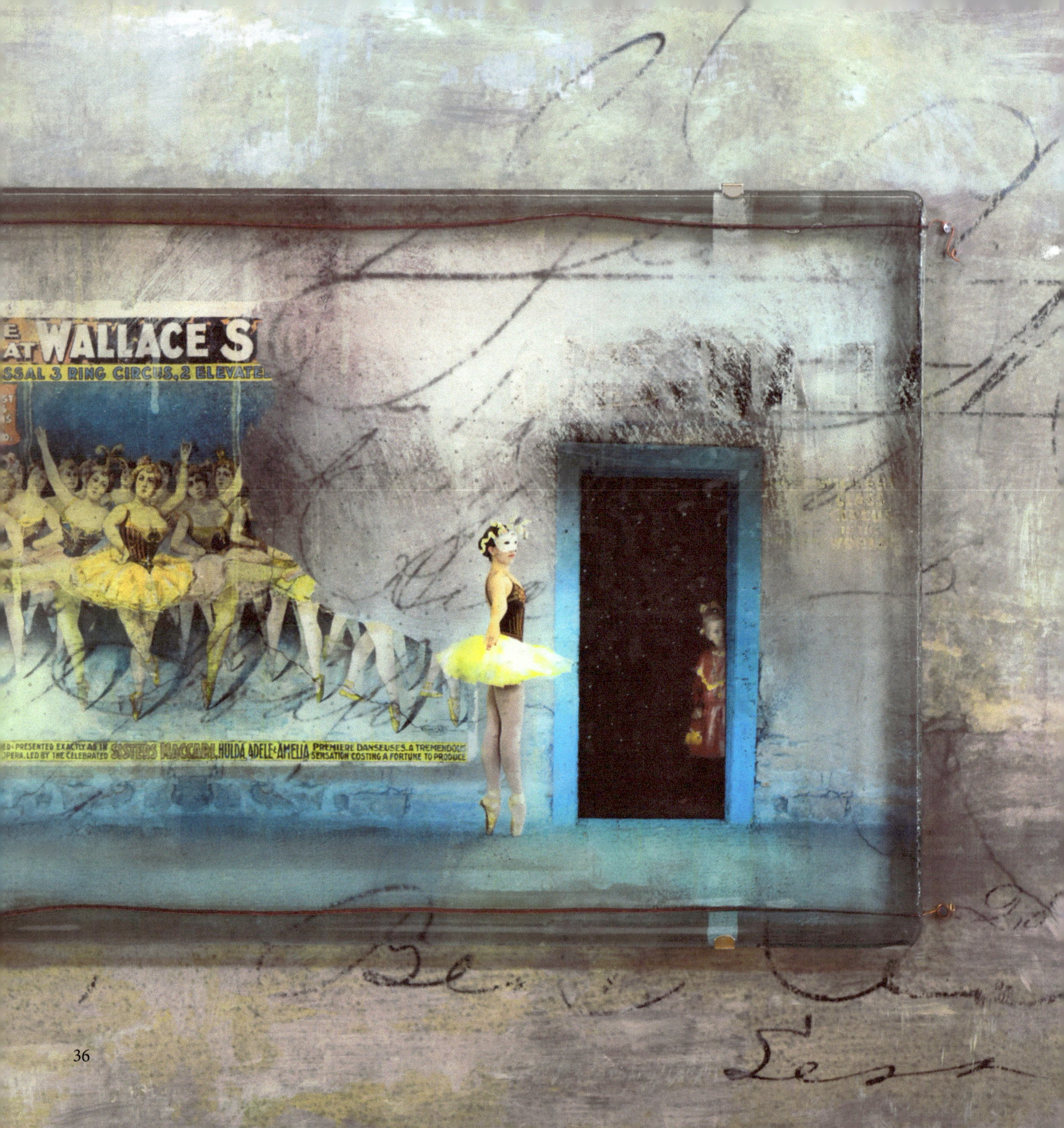
WALLACE S
3 RING CIRCUS, 2
PRESENTED EXACTLY AS IN
LED BY THE CELEBRATED
SISTERS MACCARI, HULDA, ADELE & AMELIA
PREMIERE DANSEUSES, A TREMENDOUS
SENSATION COSTING A FORTUNE TO PRODUCE

Magical Moment

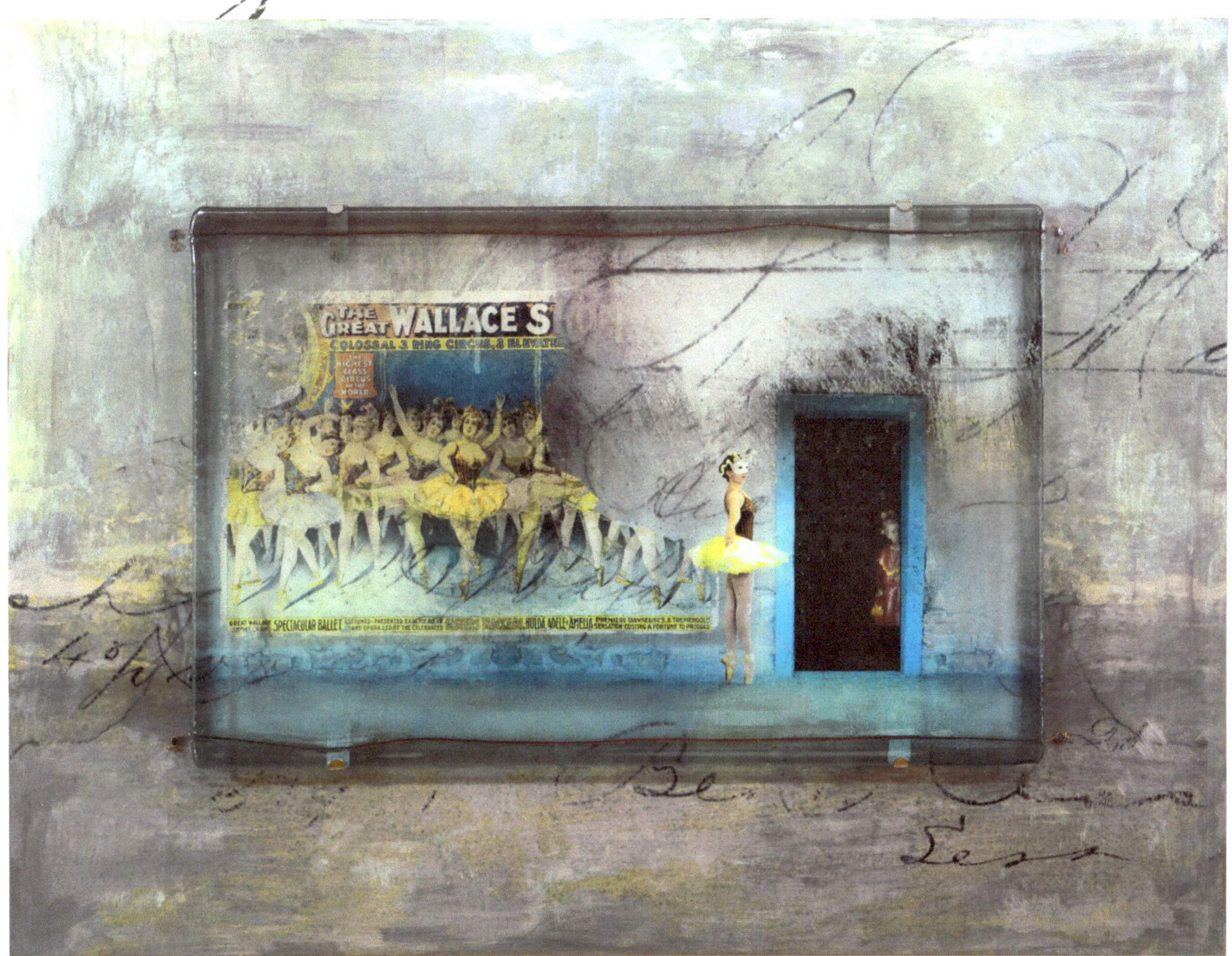

Magical Moment

Sandy Young
mixed media with kiln-formed glass, wire, tacks, on birch panel
30" x 40" x 2.5" (2013)

In *Magical Moment*, a little girl witnesses a show poster coming to life as a dancer emerges from the poster to dance in front of her.

Left: Detail of "Magical Moment".

Leaving the Ball

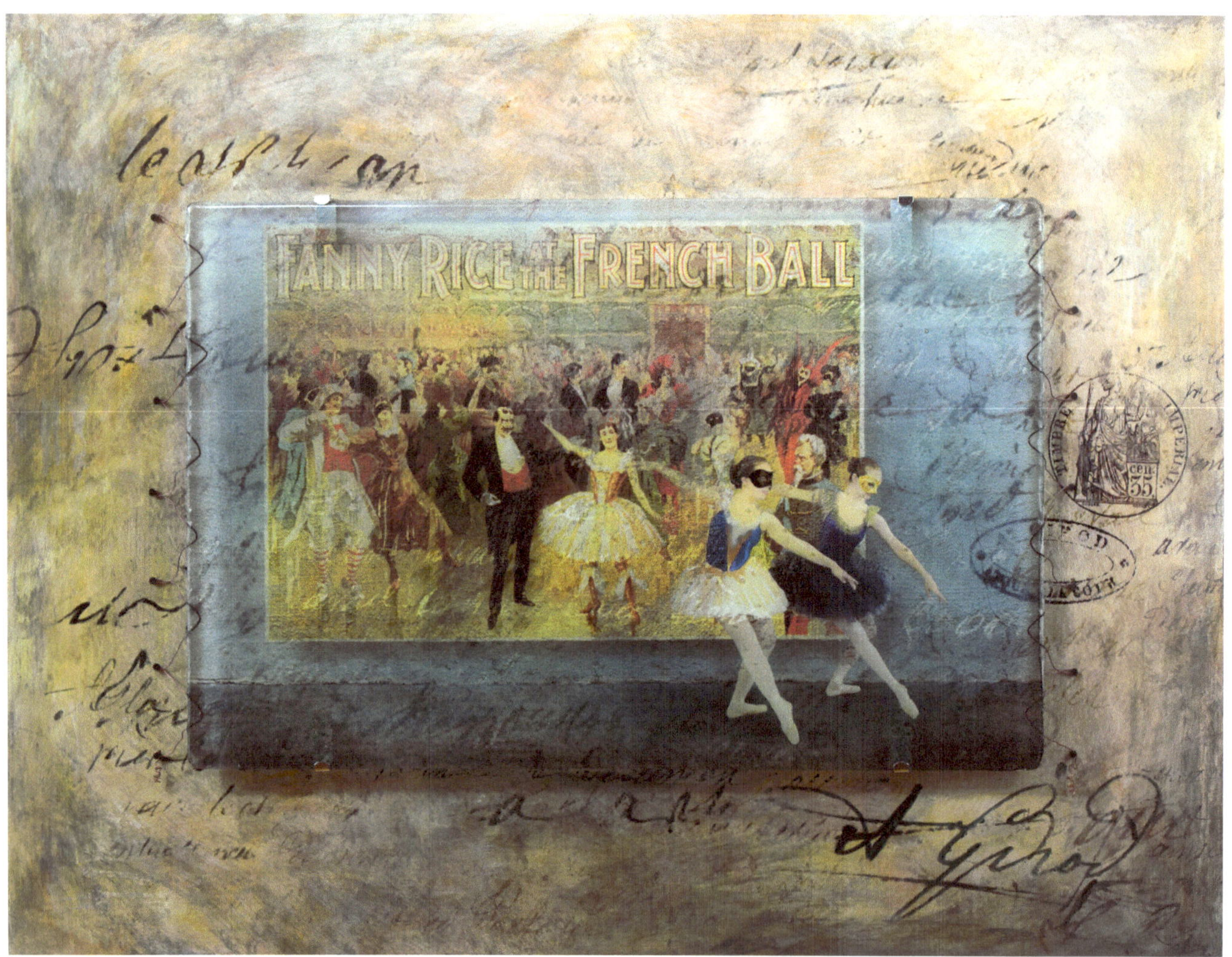

Leaving the Ball
Sandy Young
mixed media with kiln-formed glass,
wire, tacks, on birch panel
30" x 40" x 2" (2013)

In *Leaving the Ball*, two dancers "escape" from a poster advertising a show called "Fanny Rice at the French Ball".

Right: Detail of "Leaving the Ball".

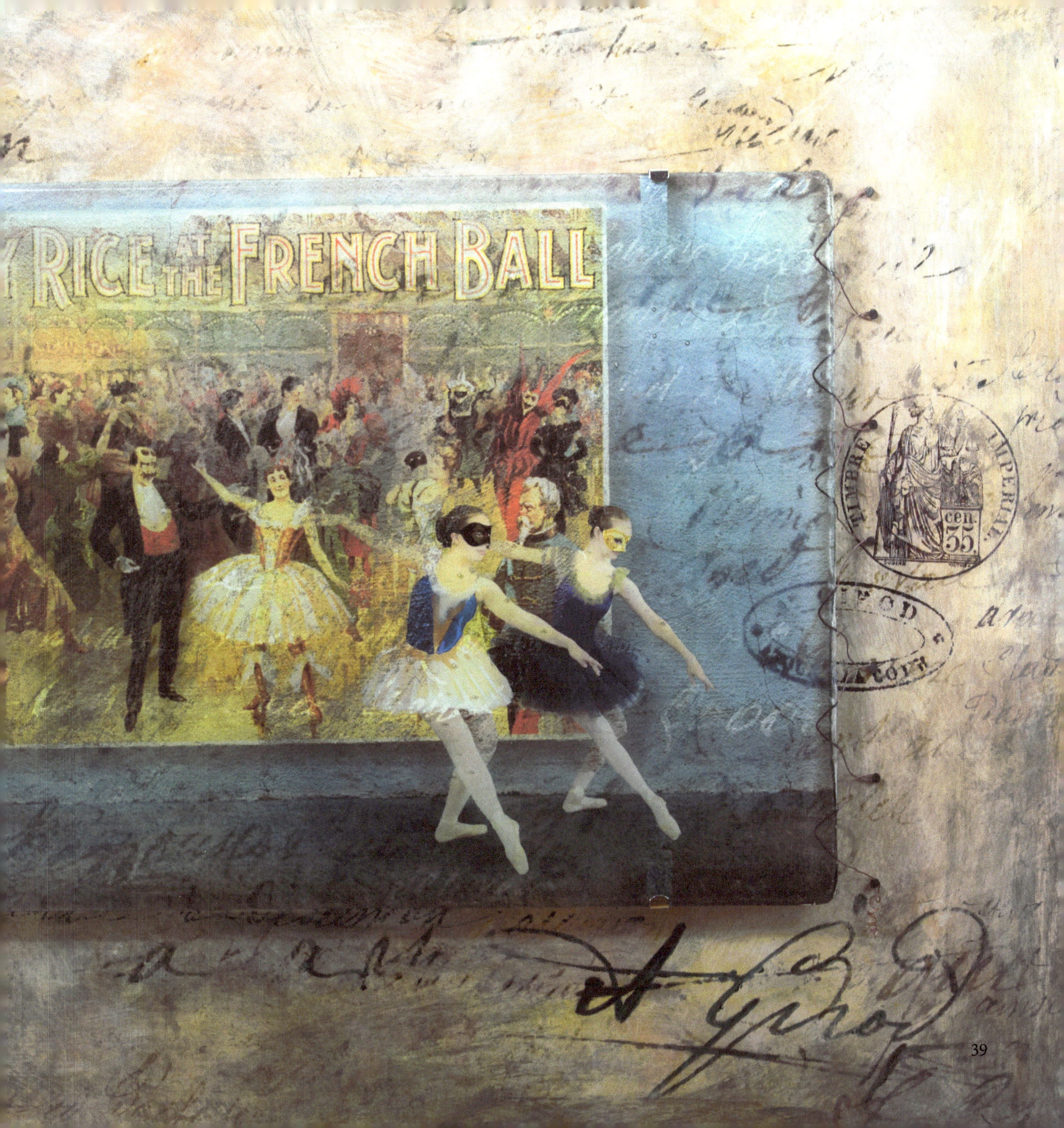
RICE AT THE FRENCH BALL
TIMBRE IMPERIAL
cen. 35

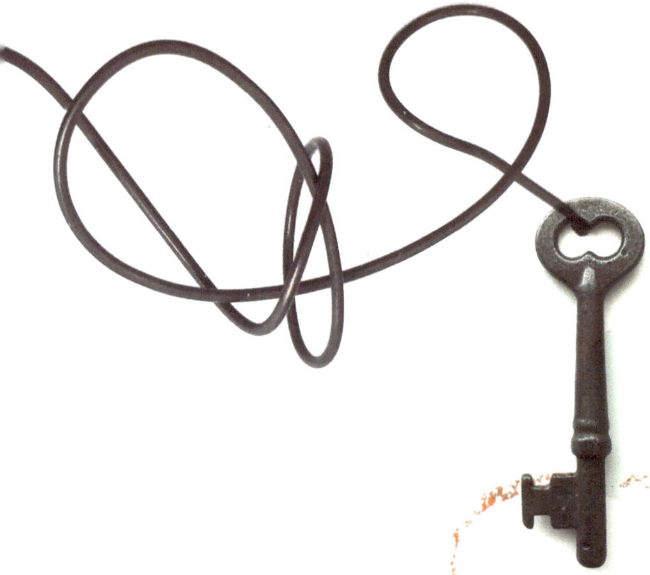

town

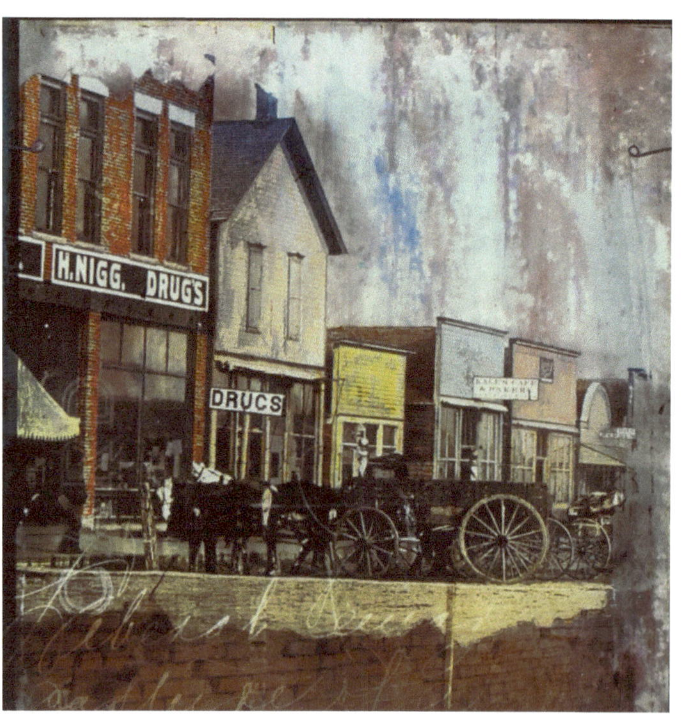

Western Town

Sandy Young

mixed media with kiln-formed glass, antique key, wire, tacks, on birch panel
36" x 24" x 2" (2014)

Left: Detail of "Western Town" glass panel. Imagery in, on and beneath the glass panel combine to form a dimensional scene.

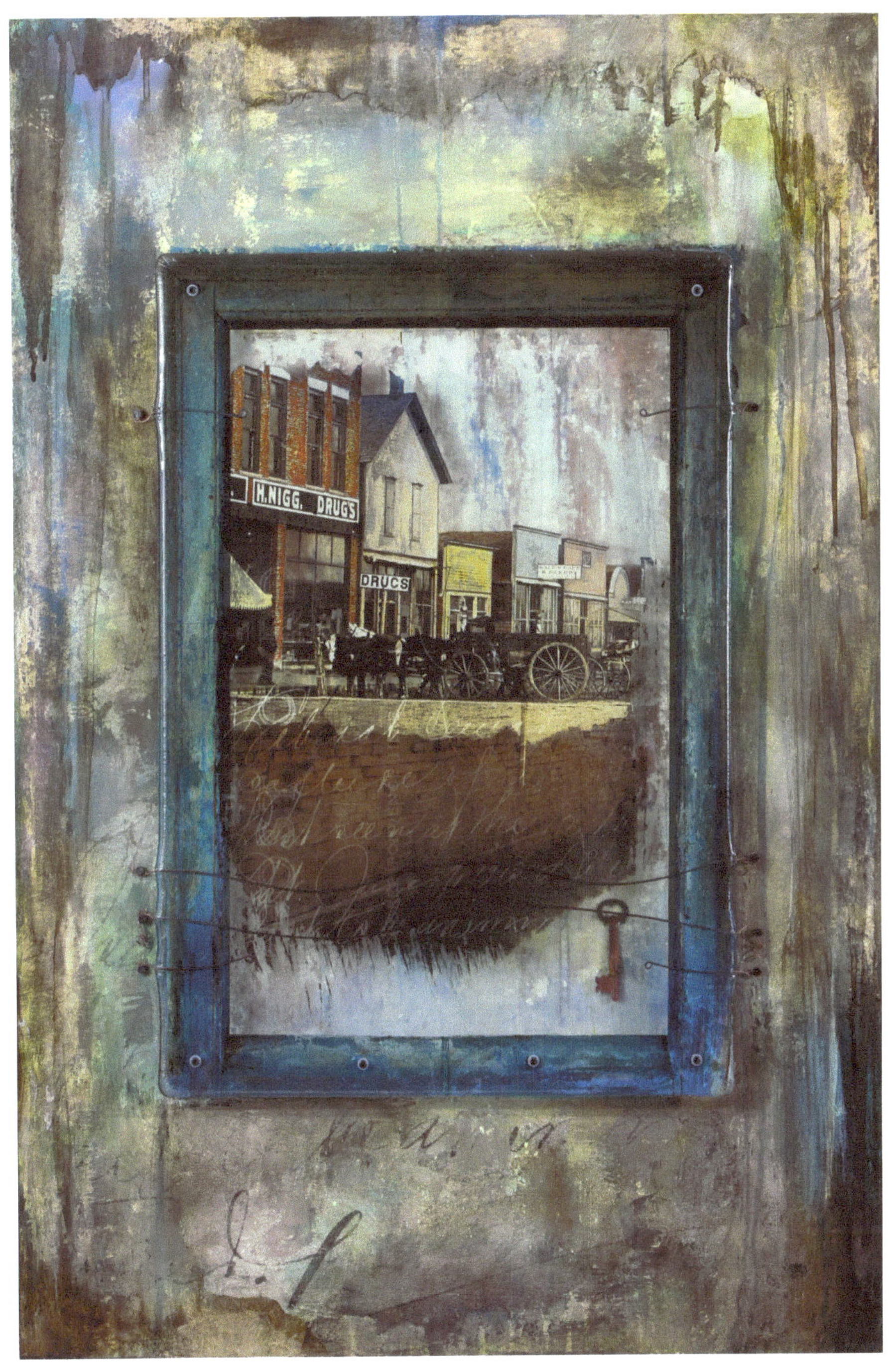
H.NIGG. DRUGS
DRUGS

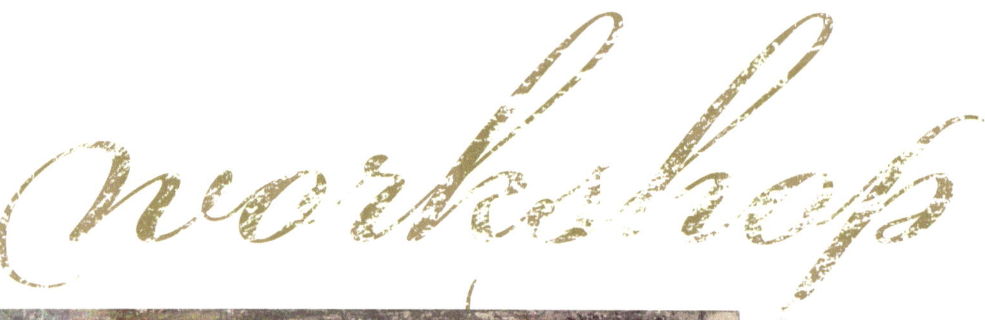

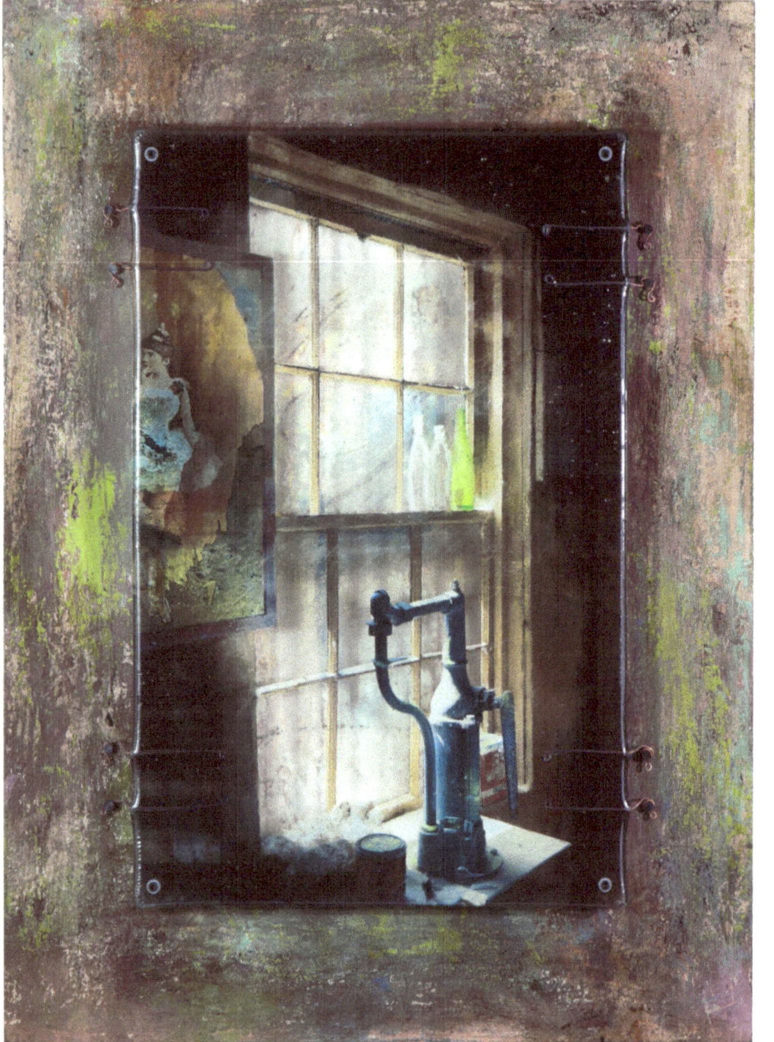

< Workshop

Sandy Young
mixed media with kiln-formed glass,
wire, tacks, on birch panel
24" x 18" x 1" (2014)

> Out West

Sandy Young
mixed media with kiln-formed glass,
antique key, wire, tacks, on birch panel
18" x 24" x 3" (2014)

O*ut West* was inspired by an actual "wanted" notice. Although not apparent in the photograph, there is much depth to this piece. The glass overlay is convex, creating a three inch gap between the center window and the scene on the back panel.

out west

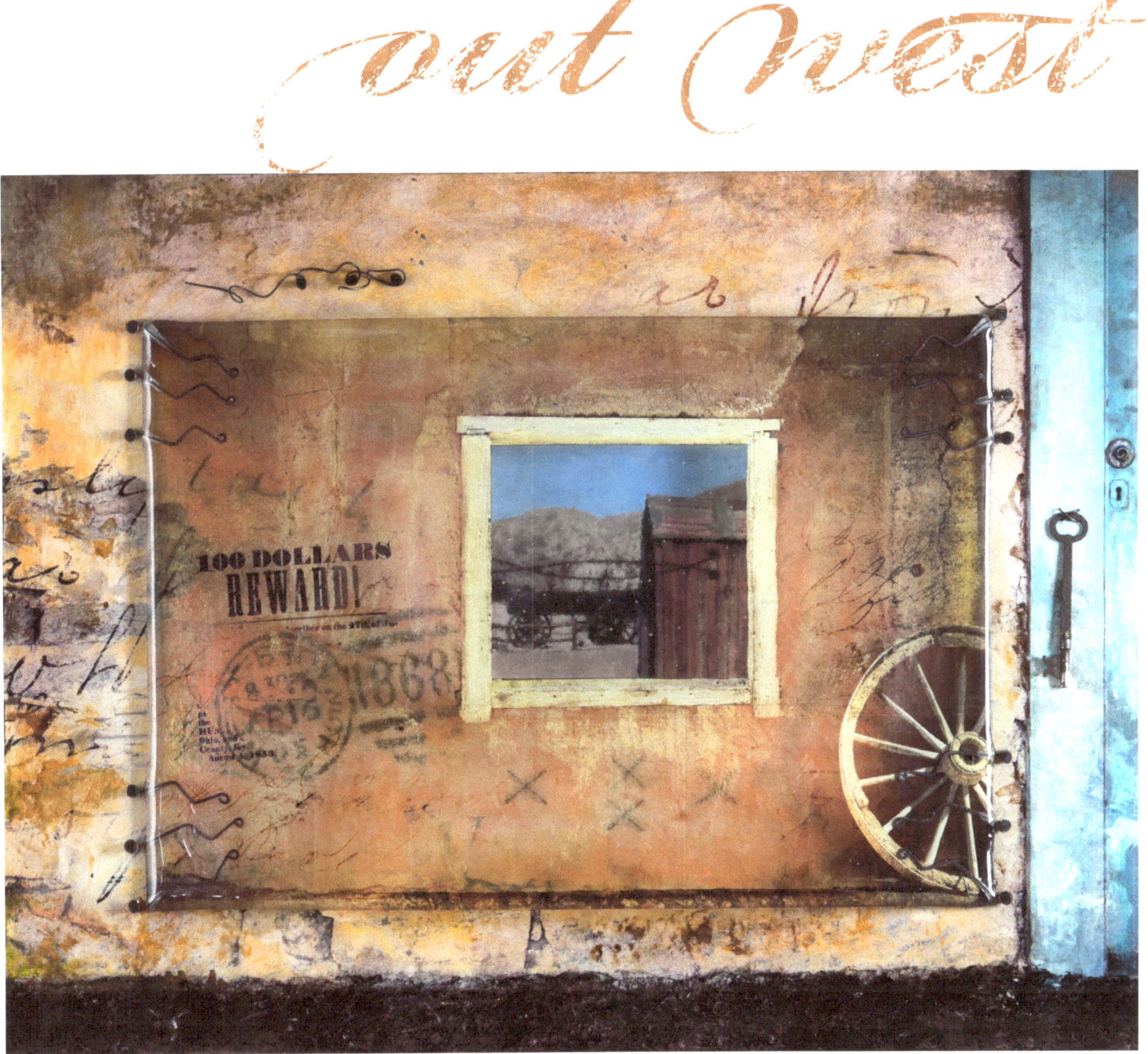

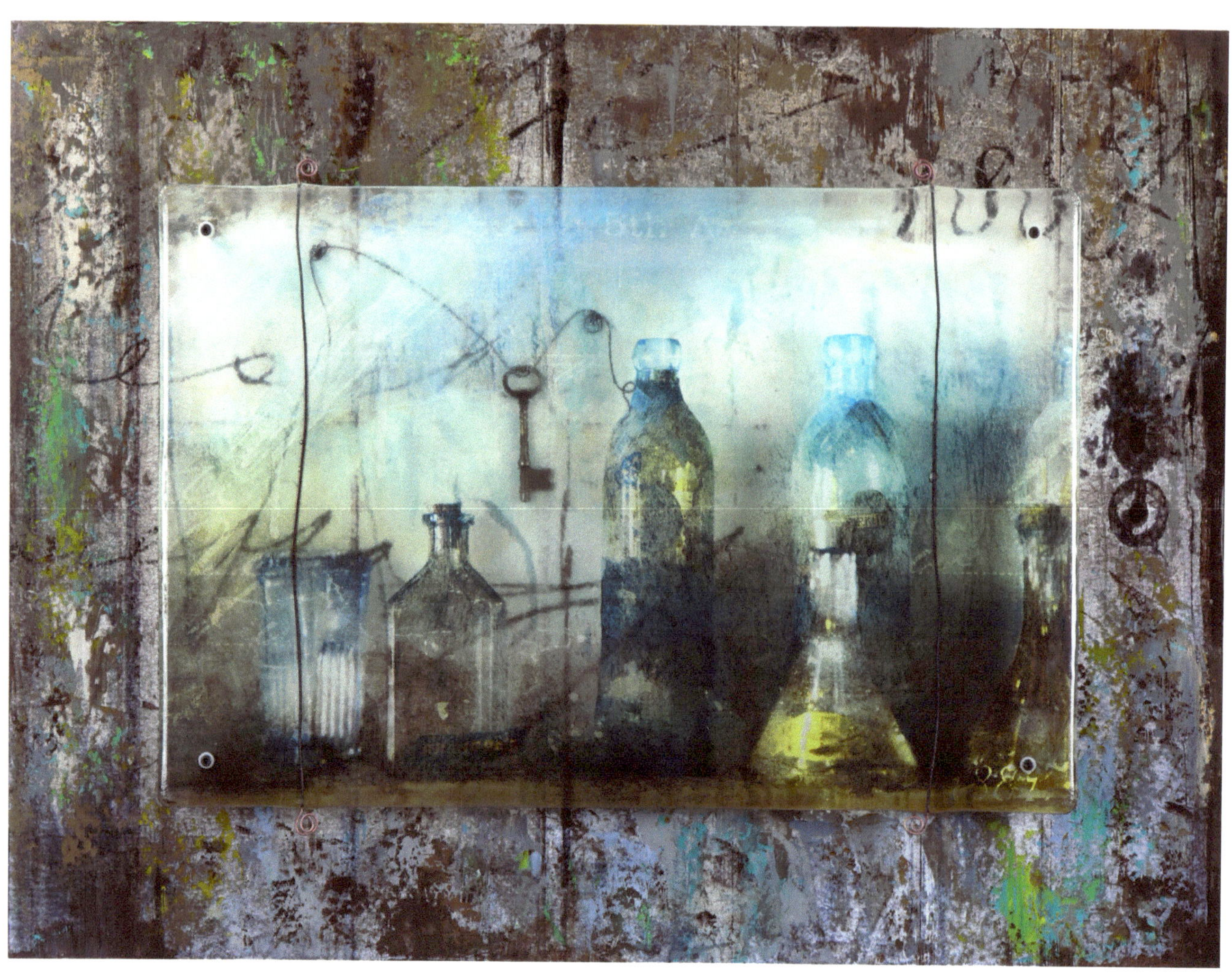

Top Shelf

Sandy Young

mixed media with kiln-formed glass, antique key, wire, tacks, on birch panel
18” x 24” x 2” (2015)

Top Shelf

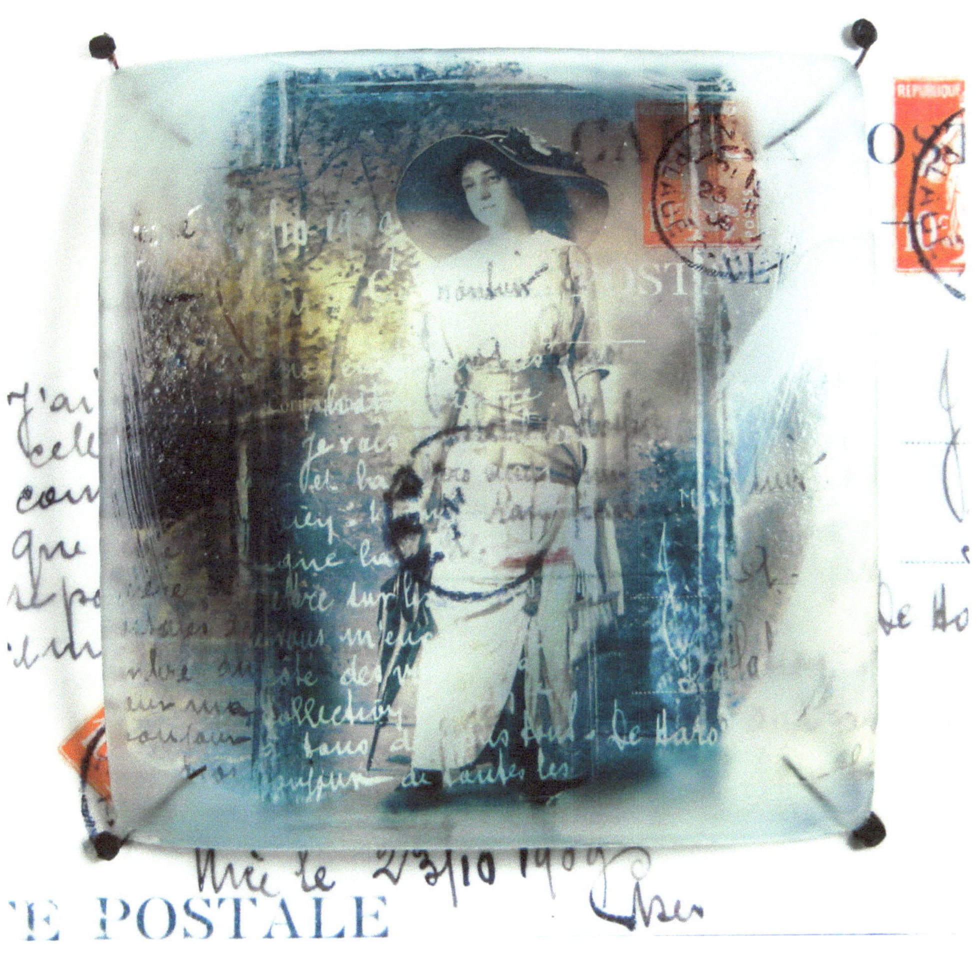

Ready to Go

Sandy Young
mixed media with kiln-formed glass,
encaustic, wire, tacks, on birch panel
10" x 20" x 2.5" (2011)

Ready to Go

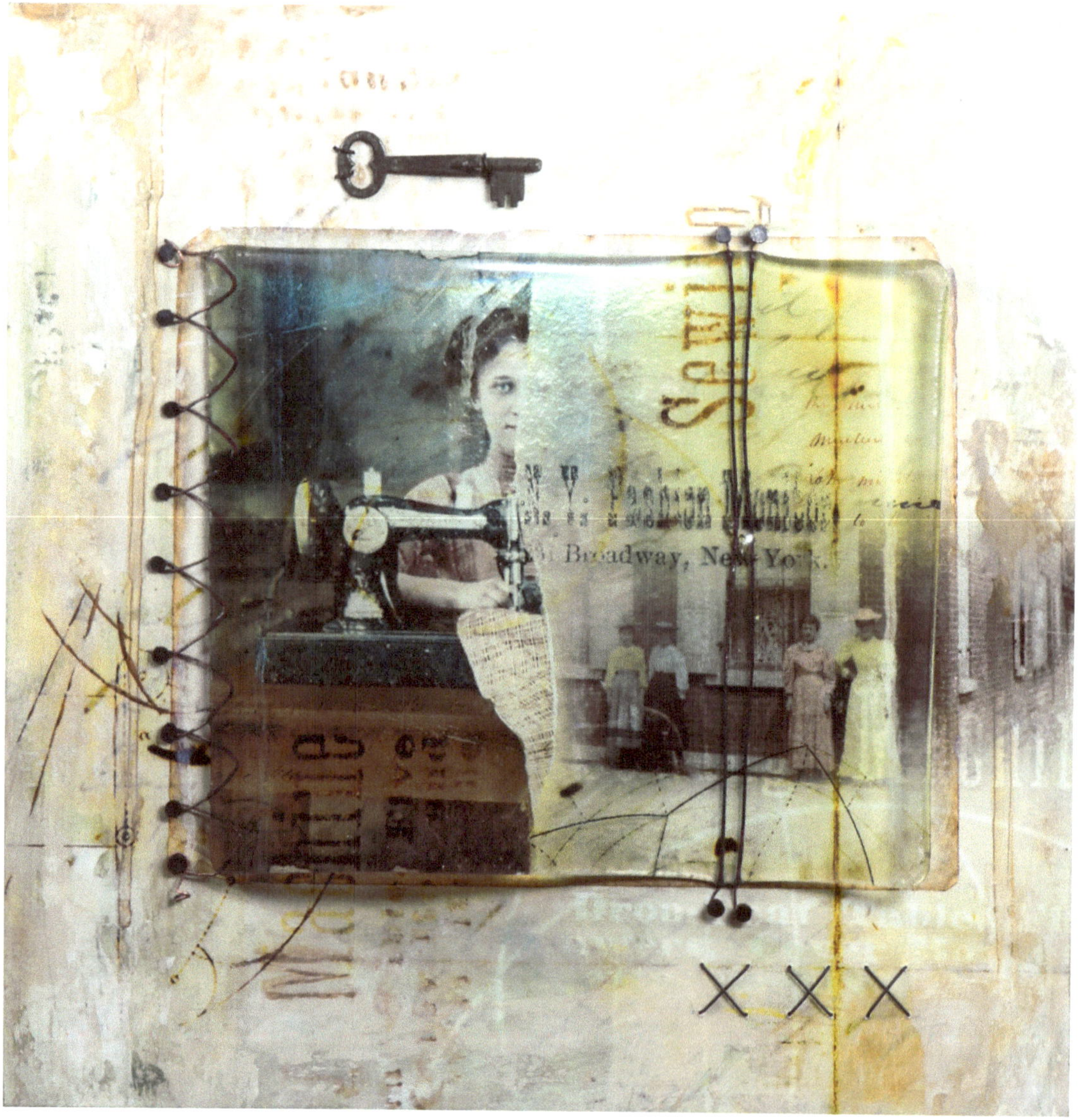

Sewing

Sandy Young

mixed media with kiln-formed glass, antique key, wire, tacks, on birch panel

14" x 14" x 2" (2015)

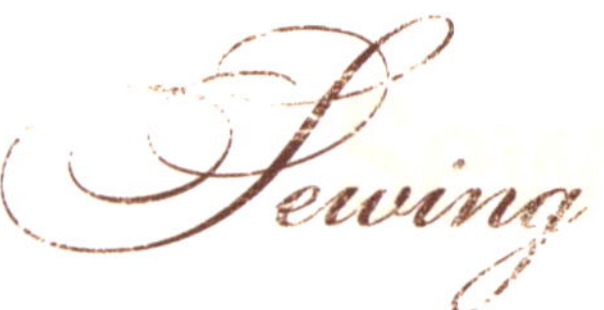

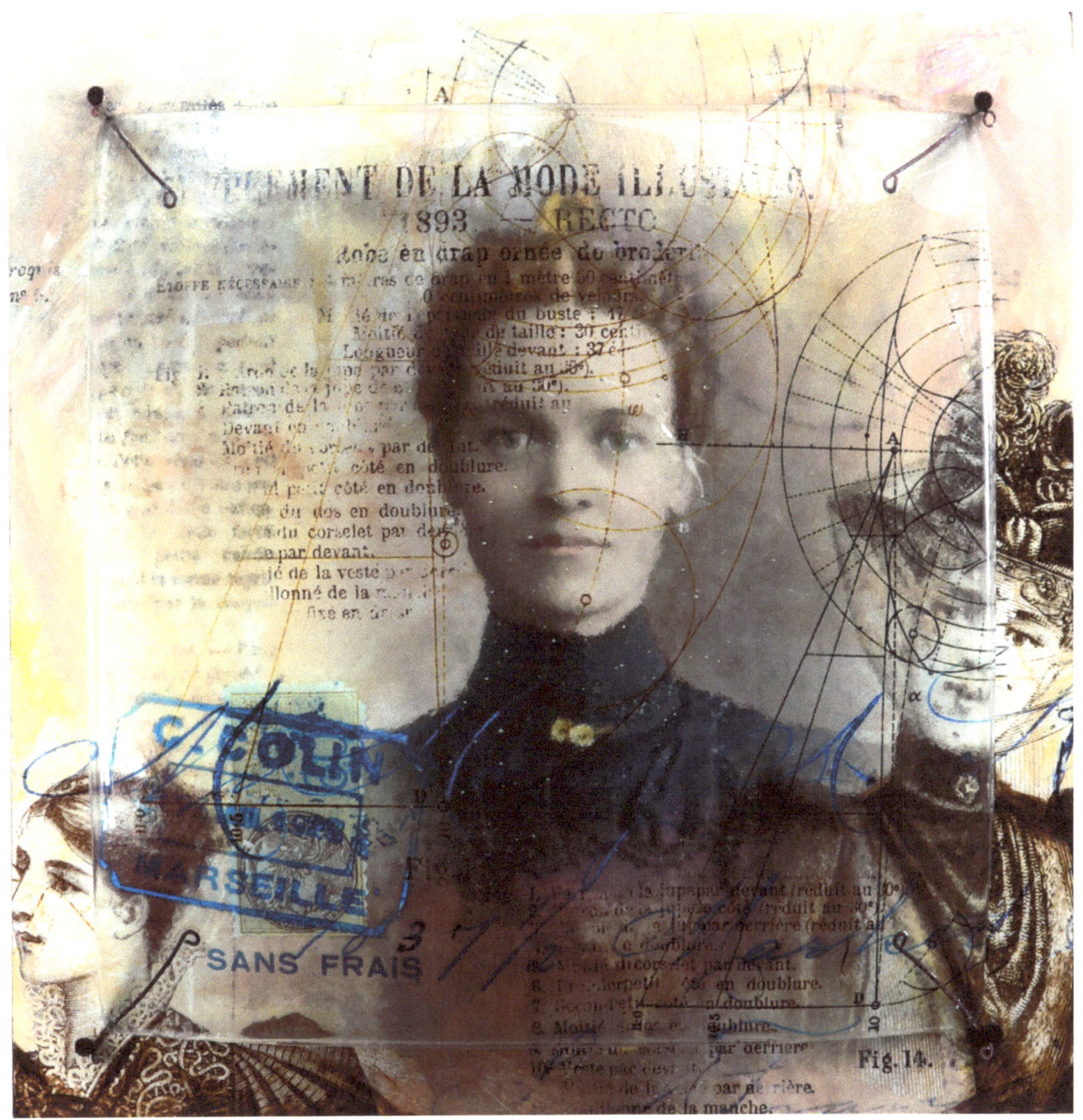

Patterns

Patterns

Sandy Young

mixed media with kiln-formed glass, wire, tacks, on birch panel

14” x 14” x 3” (2015)

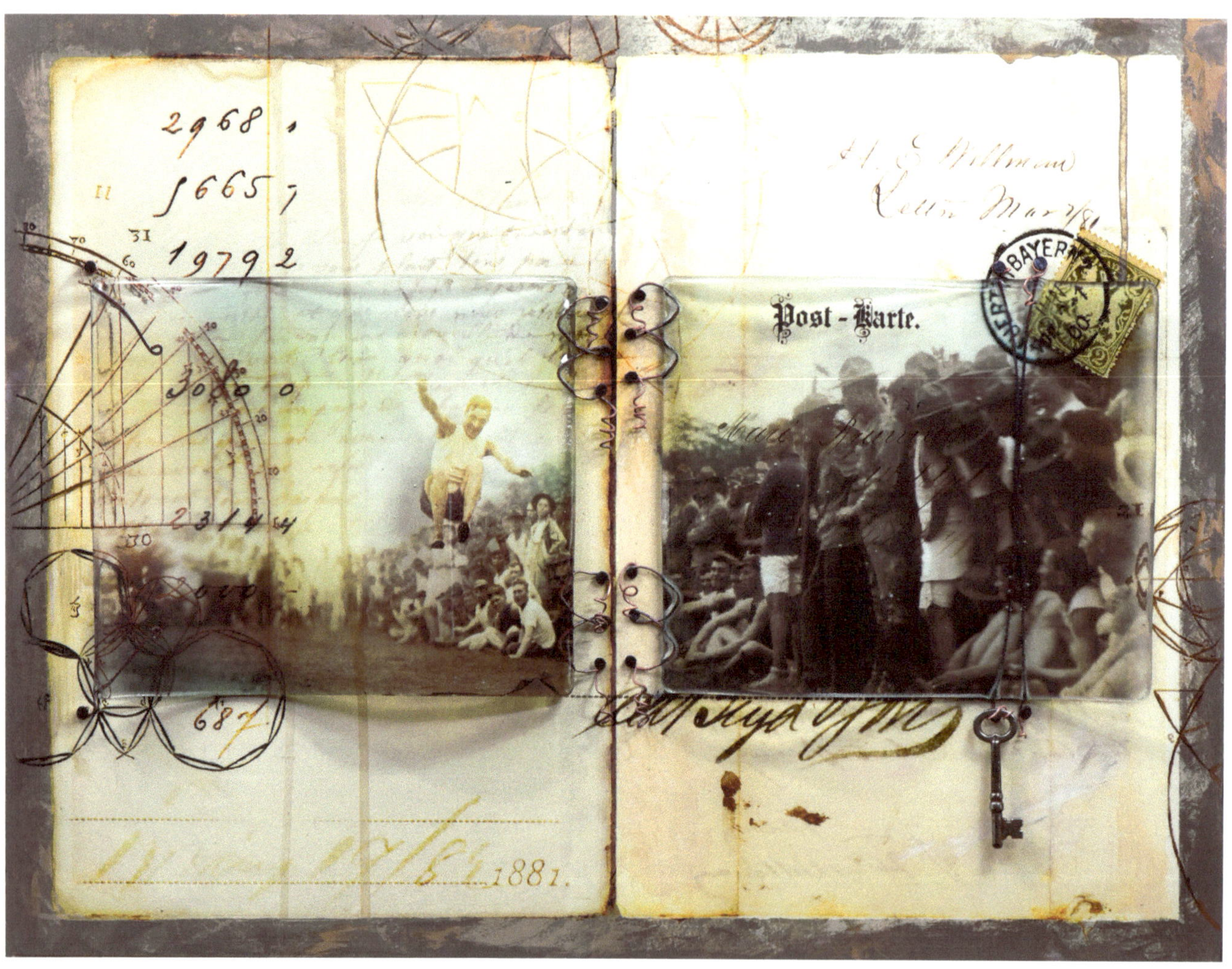
Post - Karte.
1881.

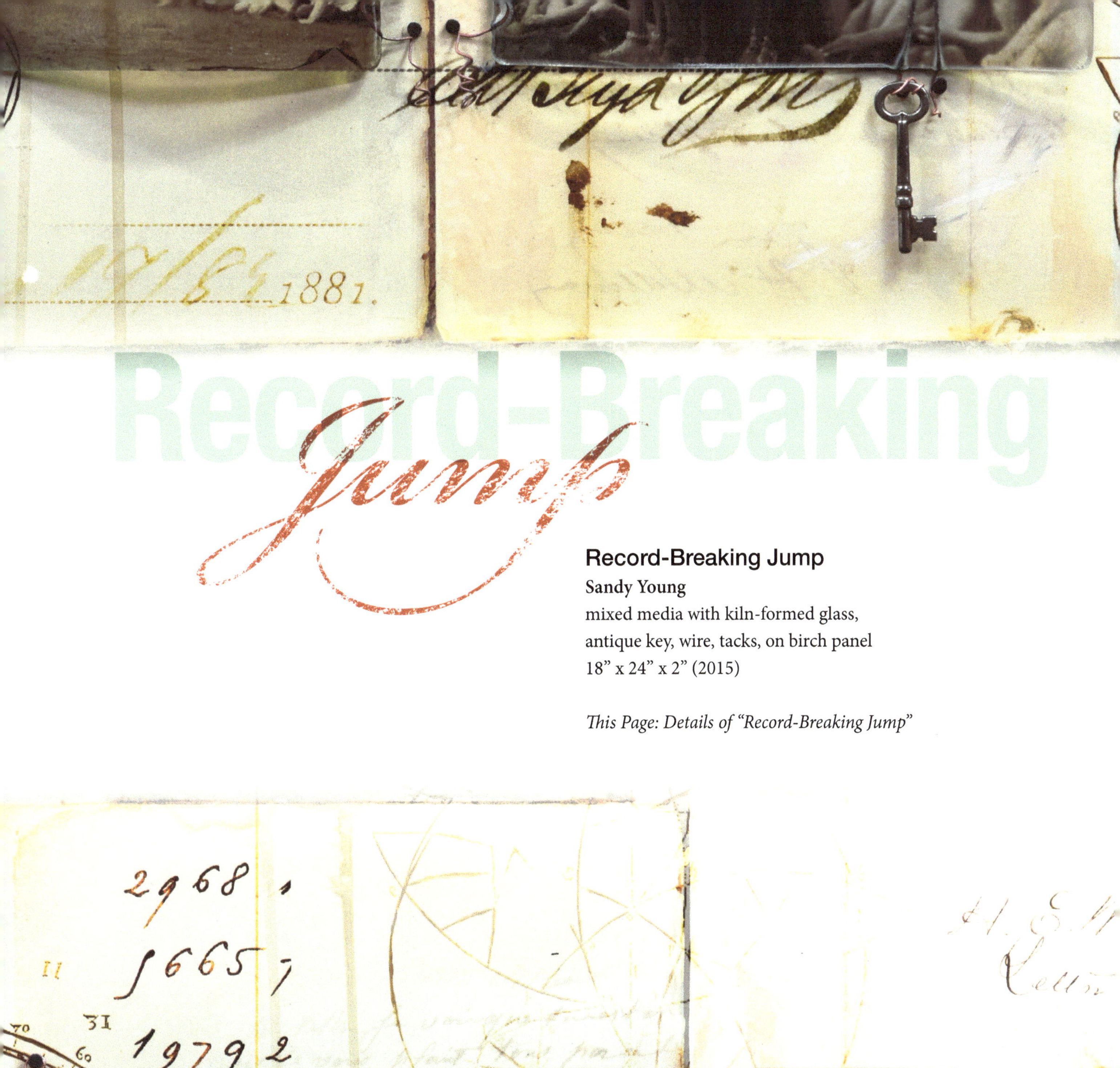

Record-Breaking Jump

Record-Breaking Jump
Sandy Young
mixed media with kiln-formed glass,
antique key, wire, tacks, on birch panel
18” x 24” x 2” (2015)

This Page: Details of “Record-Breaking Jump”

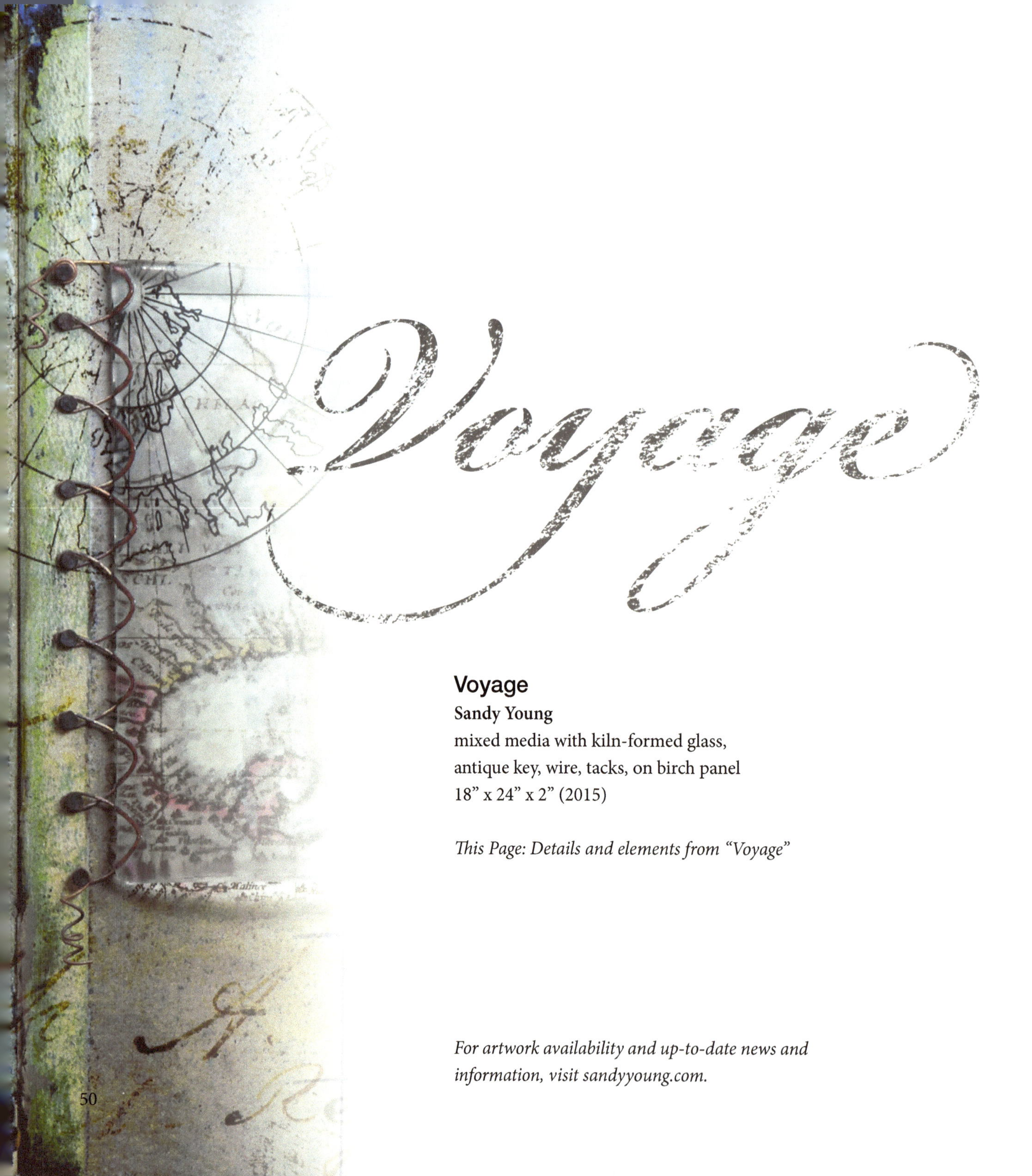

Voyage

Sandy Young

mixed media with kiln-formed glass,
antique key, wire, tacks, on birch panel
18” x 24” x 2” (2015)

This Page: Details and elements from “Voyage”

For artwork availability and up-to-date news and information, visit sandyyoung.com.

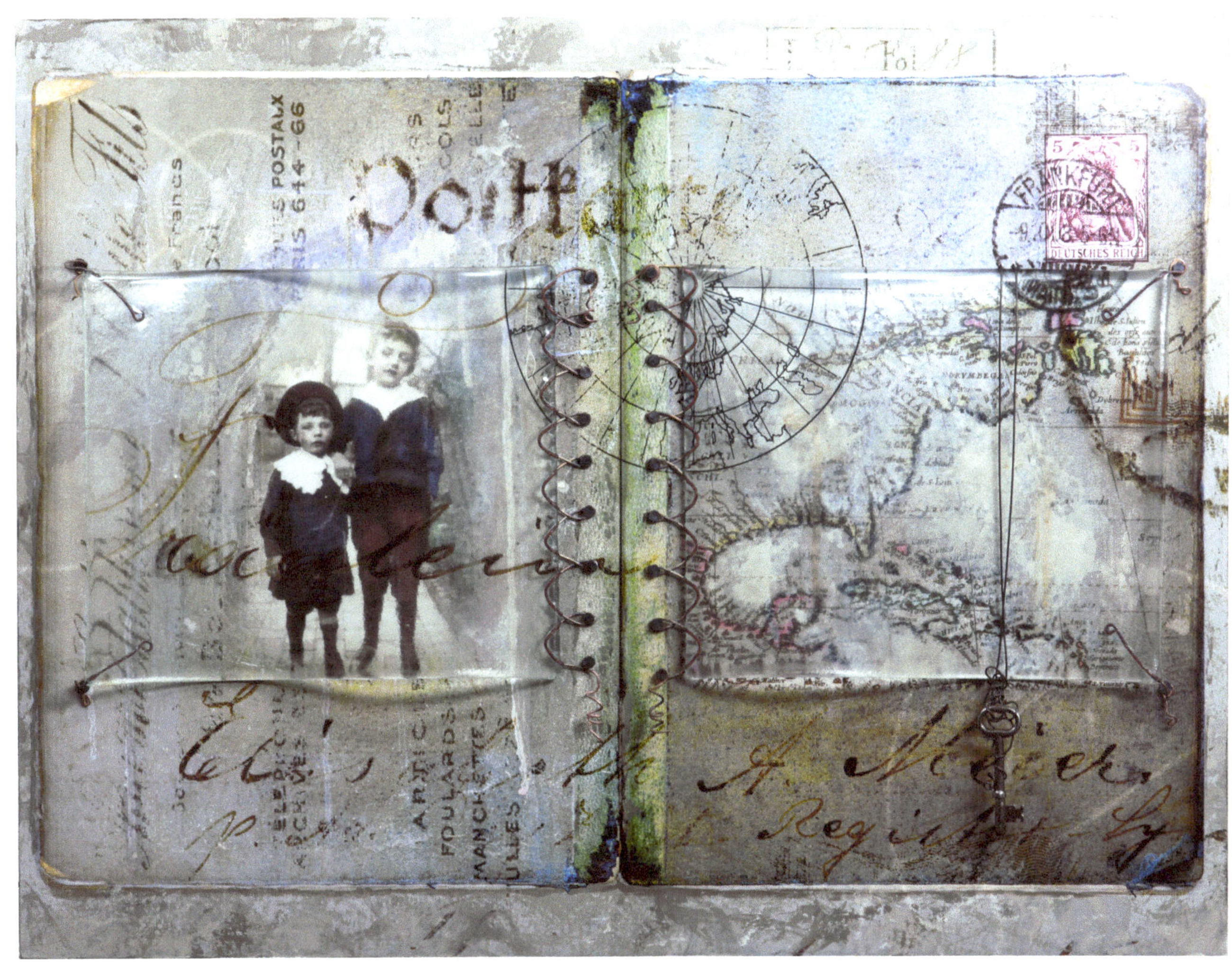
POSTAUX
FOULARDS
MANCHETTES
DEUTSCHES REICH

next?

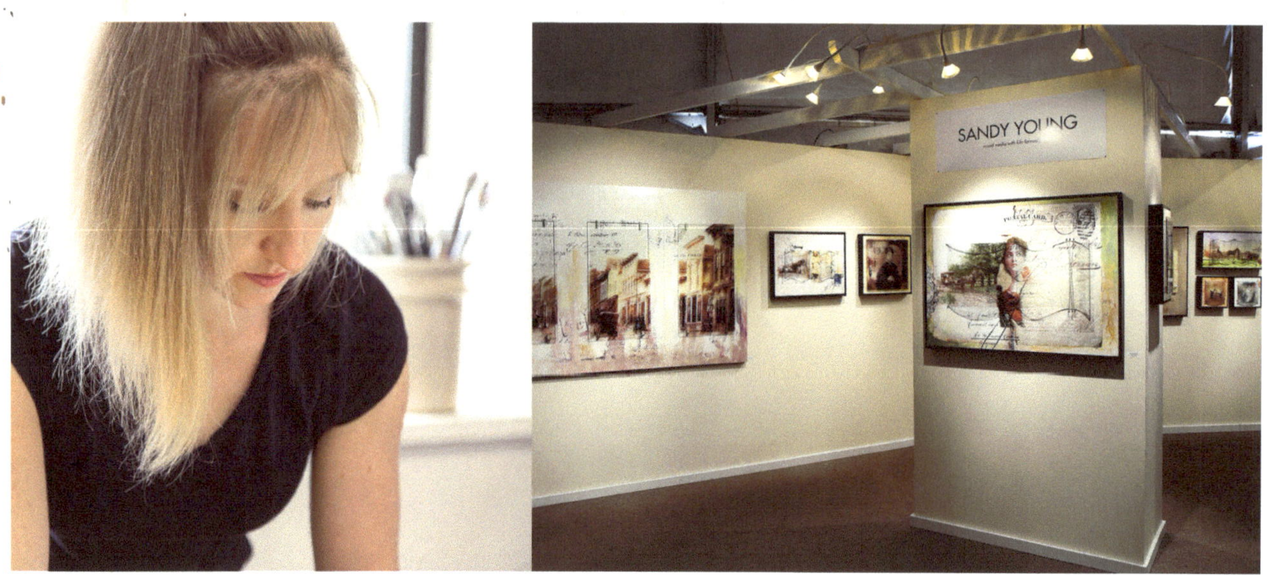

I hope you have enjoyed your journey through the artworks of *Postcard Memories*. I am grateful to all who appreciate my work. Thank you.

The best way to find out what's next, or to receive notice about shows and the release of my next art book is to sign up for my mailing list at **www.sandyyoung.com**.

Updates and information:
www.sandyyoung.com
facebook.com/sandyyoungArt
instagram.com/sandyyoungart

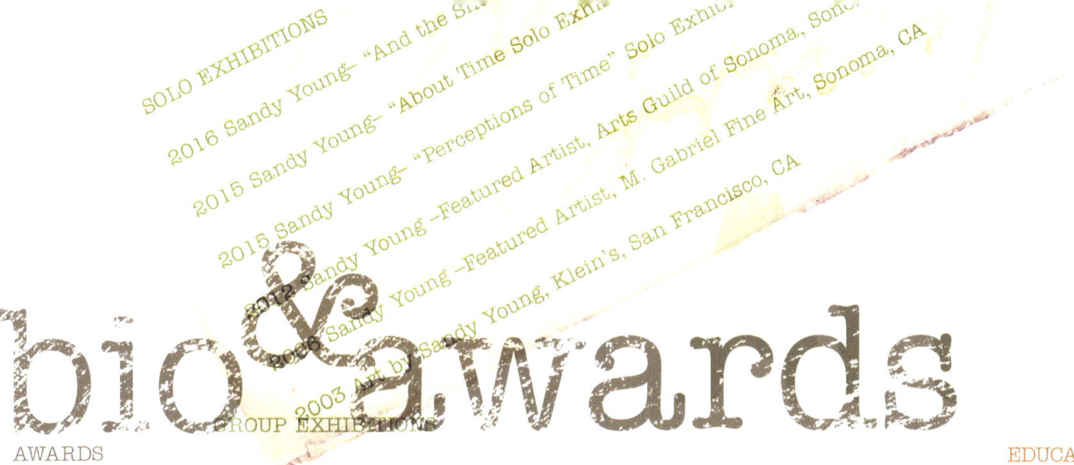

AWARDS

2017 Third Place, Altered Book & Book Arts Exhibition, Marin Museum of Contemporary Art
2017 Third Place, Hidden, Marin Museum of Contemporary Art
2013 Best of Show, ABZ Etcetera, Sebastopol Center for the Arts
2012 Sacramento Fine Arts Center Award
2012 Merit Award, California Fine Art, California State Fair
1998 First Place, New Media Art, Sausalito Art Festival
1998 Merit Award, California Works, California State Fair
1998 Second Place, Art & Science Collaborations, Inc. (ASCI)
1998 Honorable Mention, Digital Print Exhibition, California Museum of Art
1998 Merit Award, L'eau Exhibition, San Francisco Women Artists Gallery
1997 First Place, New Media Art, Sausalito Art Festival
1996 Top 10 Award (from almost 1500 entries), Digital Design Art
1996 Second Place, New Media Art, Sausalito Art Festival
1996 Merit Award, Winds of Change Exhibition, San Francisco Women Artists Gallery
1995 Merit Award, Small Format Exhibition, San Francisco Women Artists Gallery

GROUP EXHIBITIONS

2017 The Art of the Book, Seager Gray Gallery, Mill Valley, CA
2017 Art Market San Francisco, Represented by Seager Gray Gallery, San Francisco, CA
2017 Altered Book & Book Arts, Marin Museum of Contemporary Art, Novato, CA
2017 Hidden, Marin Museum of Contemporary Art, Novato, CA
2016 Palm Springs Art Fair, Represented by Sandra Lee Gallery, Palm Springs, CA
2015 Group Show, Sandra Lee Gallery, San Francisco, CA
2015 Sausalito Art Festival, Sausalito, CA
2015 Art Silicon Valley, Represented by Sandra Lee Gallery, San Mateo, CA
2015 LA Art Show, Represented by Sandra Lee Gallery, Los Angeles, CA
2015 Celebration of Fine Art, Scottsdale, AZ
2014 Group Show, Sandra Lee Gallery, San Francisco, CA
2014 Silicon Valley Contemporary, Represented by Sandra Lee Gallery, San Jose, CA
2014 Sausalito Art Festival, Sausalito, CA
2014 Celebration of Fine Art, Scottsdale, AZ
2013 December Invitational Show, Arts Guild of Sonoma, Sonoma, CA
2013 Group Show, Eminent Design Gallery, Sonoma, CA
2013 ABZ Etcetera, Sebastopol Center fr the Arts, Sebastopol, CA
2013 Celebration of Fine Art, Scottsdale, AZ
2012 California Fine Art, Sacramento, CA

EDUCATION

Printmaking Courses, University o
One year Full Fellowship, Stanford
B.S. "Materials, Techniques & Forn
Artists & Technology Series, MIT C

LITERATURE

2017 The Art of the Book, 12th Annual E
2003 Writing with Images: Toward a Sem
University of Washington, 2003
2002 Photoshop 7 Magic, & Lo
2001 Pixel Perfect, Edited by Kathleen Z
Also published worlwide by Nippon Shup
1998 WIRED News, "It's Digital, But is it
1997 Painter 5 F/X, London, Grossman &
1997 PRINT Magazine 1997 Art & Desig
1997 Design Graphics Magazine, Australi
1997 MAC Art & Design Quarterly Maga
1997 A Review by Jonathan Bock: The 4

complete & legible bio:
sandyyoung.com

www.ingramcontent.com/pod-product-compliance
Ingram Content Group UK Ltd.
Pitfield, Milton Keynes, MK11 3LW, UK
UKHW060111300726
14090UKWH00002B/133

9780999325001